The Road

Guide to

Scotland and Ireland

Dick Henneman

Panther Publishing

First published by Panther Publishing Ltd in 2004
Panther Publishing Ltd, 10 Lime Avenue, High Wycombe, Bucks. HP11 1DP, UK

Acknowledgements
I'd like to thank all those who knowingly or unknowingly have helped me in the preparation of this guide. In particular to my wife Shirley and our daughter Jo who have accompanied me on many of the routes, and to Roger, Mark, Shaz, Simon and Rob who have all put up with my disappearing down unmarked roads just to find out 'what it's like down there'. They've all suffered many a U-turn as a consequence. And thanks too to Ron Brett and Brettours who kindled my enthusiasm for long distance touring and exploring all those hard to find roads and places.
Dick Henneman

ISBN 0 9535098 7 7

Contents

About This Guide

This is a touring guide book for motorcyclists. If you enjoy getting about on two-wheels, whether it's on a tourer, a traillie, a sportsbike, a cruiser or a classic, then you can go touring. And in spite of all the speed restrictions, Gatso cameras and general traffic mayhem, when you get to Scotland and Ireland there are some great roads for the motorcyclist to ride.

If your idea of travelling is finding the most interesting way from A to B, with good demanding riding, places to take a break along the way, and excellent scenery, then this is a book for you. But if you're more interested in how quickly you can get to B and what you'll find when you get there, then you'd be better off reading one of the more 'conventional' guide books.

This book is intended to persuade you to go touring, and once you've tried it I've no doubt that you'll want to go back for more. So as well as information on the variety of features in the country itself, I've included sections on preparation for both yourself and the bike, how to get there (and back) on two wheels, and the types of accommodation that are available and how to book. But most important of all, there are details and routes for some of the best and most interesting roads and routes for you to ride.

This is the first edition of the guide, and everything in it is based upon my own experiences. However, in an area the size of Scotland and Ireland things are constantly changing and nothing in the guide should be taken as a guarantee that what you'll find is exactly as described. In particular, road works and improvements are common and may make some of the routes out-of-date before they can be put in print. You can help me here, by letting me know what you find 'on the ground' and I'll then incorporate this in the next edition. In addition, if you find some great routes or services and facilities that would help other motorcyclists then I'd like to hear about these as well.

Enjoy!

Dick Henneman

October 2003

YOUR INTRODUCTION TO SCOTLAND AND IRELAND

Ireland is split into two parts. Northern Ireland is a part of the United Kingdom whereas the south of Ireland (Eire) is a separate country within the European Union. Scotland, like Northern Ireland is a part of the United Kingdom, a collection of islands and countries, perched above France and surrounded by the North Sea, the English Channel and the North Atlantic. The UK and Eire cover an area of some 146,000 sq. miles (378,900 sq. km.), and Scotland and Ireland occupy some 43% of this landmass, but are only home to around 18% of the total population. This means that in Scotland and Ireland things generally only get busy on the roads near the main centres of population but are otherwise mercifully free of traffic.

Scotland and Ireland have a large number of roads that are a pleasure to ride and explore from the seat of a motorbike. All you need is a little bit of local knowledge and some forward planning, and that's where this guide can help. In it I've collected some of the roads that I've enjoyed riding, either for the scenery that they pass through, or the dynamics of the riding itself, or sometimes both. But this is not a definitive list. I have largely confined the routes in this first edition of the guide to the southern half of Ireland and the more accessible parts of Scotland but that does not mean there are not excellent roads to ride in the other regions of these two countries. There are some great roads that I've ridden that I'm not going to tell you about – well, not just yet anyway – and there are a lot more out there just waiting for you to discover. So get out there.

A POTTED HISTORY

So how did Scotland and Ireland get to be the way they are now? As the glaciers retreated from the landscape for the last time some 10,000 years ago, Stone Age men pushed trails though the virgin forests that advanced in the wake of the ice. These early Britons came across the land bridge that joined the country to the rest of continental Europe, until the North Sea broke through some 3,000 years later. Neolithic invaders from the Mediterranean lands replaced Stone Age man, and brought with them farming techniques, the art of pottery and the use of stone. They worked flints and were buried in long barrows, which are scattered on the Downs across the south of England and in other parts of the country. Such settlements as existed were organised on a tribal basis and by and large each tribe got on with its own business. Later invaders brought skills in the working of bronze, and were responsible for the erection of enormous stone circles from Salisbury Plain to the Orkney Islands.

Around 500 BC came the first of many great migratory movements from the people of the continental land mass. These were the Celts, who brought with them a new technology based on the working of iron. Later Celts were

miners and traders, farmers, horse-breeders and cattle farmers, and the Celtic language they used still lives on in the Welsh tongue. These peoples were mostly absorbed into the existing tribal structures, although there were inevitably some conflicts.

The Roman invasion that began in AD 43 was not a mass migration, but an occupation by a small group of highly organised conquerors. The Romans subjugated the natives, used their resources and dominated them with superior force and administration. They even moved into Scotland under Agricola's command, defeating the Caledonians at Mons Graupius, but they never invaded Ireland. It took another 400 years before the Celts, in an alliance with Germanic raiders, broke the Roman hold and set up the first Anglo-Saxon settlements. They in turn faced the onslaught of Norse and Danish invaders who established bases in the Shetlands and Orkneys, and then spread down the west coast, finally invading Ireland in the 8th century. For the next two hundred years, the Scandinavian pirate raids did a great deal of damage to the country, but the Anglo-Norman invasion that began in 1170 completely overturned the traditional Irish way of life, and for much of the medieval period, Ireland had a feudal economy under English lordship.

Meanwhile, in Scotland the four tribes of Picts, Scots, British and Angles had united to form the kingdom of Scotland under its first king, Duncan. But these were violent times and very few of the early Scottish kings died of old age. Relations with England were also far from friendly in spite of the anglicisation of the church and the administration, and it wasn't until 1603 when James VI of Scotland became James I of England that things quietened down. However, in Ireland the divisions were deepening. A series of wars and the effects of the Reformation had resulted in a country that was essentially Catholic, but ruled by an English-speaking and Protestant government. The country was being slowly impoverished by legislation, and by the 19th century was largely operating at subsistence levels with all the power being wielded from England.

In Scotland, Edinburgh and Glasgow were rapidly developing cities while the countryside was still relatively poor. Recent innovations in agriculture and industry had given a massive boost to the country's economy, but at a price to its social structure. Land enclosures had depopulated the Highlands and the resulting migrations to the booming Lowland cities had resulted in overcrowded housing, slum conditions, filth and squalor. The problem was made worse by the arrival of thousands of Irish immigrants fleeing the famine conditions in their country.

The Great Famine of 1846-7 was seen by many Irish to be the direct result of English rule, and was largely responsible for the creation of the Fenian movement to restore the country's political freedom. The English finally woke up to the need for this towards the end of the 19th century, but the Home Rule bills were too little, too late in the face of the formation of Sinn Fein (Ourselves Alone) from the Fenians, and the Ulster Unionists from the largely Protestant counties around Belfast. Things came to a head in 1916 with the Easter Uprising, and for the next four years the Irish Republican Army fought a guerilla war against military and government targets. In 1921 an attempt was made to halt the hostilities by signing the Anglo-Irish Treaty, which partitioned the country to form the Irish Free State (becoming the Republic of Ireland in 1949) and Northern Ireland.

Meanwhile, Scotland continued to develop its industrial and commercial strengths, along with its agriculture, and in the 1960s the discovery of oil and natural gas in the North Sea gave it another economic boost. Towards the end of the 20th century, Eire became the 'tiger economy' of the EU and today both countries have an active and developing tourism industry.

Geography & Geology

The variety of the British and Irish scenery is largely due to the influences of the underlying rocks. Some of these in the barren wilderness of West Sutherland in Scotland, date back around 3,400 million years and are the amongst the oldest rocks in the world; while others off the coast of Dungeness, are still in the process of being formed. But around 570 million years ago, most of what is now the UK was below a warm shallow sea and over a period of time a great thickness of mud and silt accumulated. This was compressed under later deposits, along with ash and lava from volcanoes, and then some 350 million years ago there was a major upwards earth movement which resulted in the formation of the Caledonian Mountains. The pressures that created these mountains also caused molten rock to flow into the mountain roots giving rise to granite and igneous intrusions, some of which are still visible in Snowdonia and the Lake District.

In the following Devonian period, many of these mountain uplifts were worn away by erosive forces and the area became a desert. Much red sandstone was formed about this time, before another sea incursion drowned everything out. While all this was going on, life had evolved in the seas, and the chalky remains of these tiny creatures formed thick layers of limestone. These in turn were covered by the deltas of great rivers, which then silted up, forming muddy swamps on which thick forests flourished, decayed, and were covered with mud, subsequently turning into coalfields.

The limestones that were laid down in the Jurassic period some 175 million years ago are responsible for some of Britain's best building stone and most of its iron ore. In west Scotland, the Tertiary Era which started around 65 million years ago, was marked by a new phase of volcanic activity which resulted in granites forming on the islands of Rhum, Eigg, Skye and Arran, and lava flows that formed the hexagonal columns of Fingal's Cave and the Giant's Causeway in Northern Ireland.

The last great formative action that moulded the British landscape was the Ice Age that descended from the northeast around 1 million years ago. At its greatest extent some 200,000 years ago, a permanent ice sheet covered the land as far south as a line drawn from the Thames to the mouth of the Severn. Huge tongues of ice moved out from the highlands in the north on to the lowlands of the south and east Britain. The deep trough-like valleys of the Lake District and Snowdonia were all scoured out by these glaciers, and the vast amounts of material carried by the ice sheets were spread throughout the lowlands as hummocks of sand and gravel and great sheets of thick clay. The immense mass of water from the melting of the ice sheets resulted in a rise in sea levels that eventually separated Britain and Ireland from the rest of Europe and from each other.

But the story hasn't quite finished yet. Hills and mountains are still being eroded and rivers continue to carry down material to the lowlands estuaries and the sea. The bed of the North Sea is slowly sinking under the weight of the new deposits, and the coast line of the southeast and the east coast is being continually attacked and eroded.

CLIMATE

The climate in both Scotland and Ireland can never be accused of being dull. Awful on occasions, but dull - no. Lying between the land mass of Eurasia to the east and the watery expanse of the Atlantic Ocean to the west, the British and Irish weather depends very much on what is going on in these neighbouring areas. When westerly winds blow they bring the relative mildness of the ocean atmosphere at any time of the year. Easterlies however, bring different conditions according to the season.

Despite its reputation, the Scottish and Irish climate and day-to-day weather conditions are relatively predictable. Over the Atlantic there is often a confrontation between cold airstreams moving south from the Arctic, and warm moisture-laden air moving north from the Tropics. This produces depressions - pockets of low air pressure - which move eastwards or north-eastwards across the ocean, often crossing Britain or brushing against its shores. Barometers fall, then rise again, as a mild windy and wet period is quickly followed by a warm dull spell or squally cold showers. At other times the zone of high pressure centred over the Azores expands northwards. Then, calmer air flows over the country, barometers rise and the weather is clear and sunny.

So now you're all meteorologists! But that's very much a simplification of the weather process and there's a lot of other factors that can cause considerable local variations.

Spring is normally the driest season even though April is traditionally showery. Halfway through the month the cold weather starts receding, and there are often some very warm days during the second half of the month. West-coast districts are popular for spring holidays as they are less vulnerable to rearguard actions from the winter. By late spring daytime, temperatures will have usually risen to around 21 - 24°C over a wide area. In May and June, maximum temperatures along the coasts usually exceed the sea-surface temperatures by around 5 - 9°C. This difference, at its greatest along the east coast, causes an alternation between on and offshore breezes.

June is the brightest month of the year in general, and the average daily sunshine ranges from eight hours in the extreme south, to about five hours in the north of Scotland. Rainfall tends to increase during July and August, partly because Atlantic depressions come nearer to the coasts during these months and partly because the air, as it becomes heated, is capable of holding more moisture.

Late summer is often noted for its very warm weather, and this may well continue into September with the eastern side of the country likely to be drier as the southwesterly winds will have lost a lot of their moisture as they travel across the country.

The autumn winds eventually move round to the west and northwest, and the weather becomes less settled. The air can be exceptionally clear during the sunnier spells. North and northwest winds often bring heavy falls of snow to the north of the country during late October or November, but these are usually short-lived, and when the winds subside and the sky clears the beauty of the countryside is unparalleled.

Communications

Throughout the whole of Scotland and Ireland communications are usually quite good, although in the remoter areas there may be some delays. Most of us want to keep in touch when we're away, hopefully just so we can tell everyone at home what a wonderful time we're having. But it's also a good idea to leave some contact details with friends and family, just so they can get hold of you if necessary. Try to avoid leaving contact information with your employer, unless you're among the really dedicated. After all, you are supposed to be enjoying yourself!

Postal Services

Post Office® branches can be found in most small towns, a number of villages and in the cities, and are usually red in colour. The sign to look for is a red oval enclosing the words 'Post Office' in yellow. Opening hours vary with location, but generally are from 9.00am to 16.30pm with an hour for lunch taken sometime between 12.00pm and 14.00pm. Queues can be long, so if you only want the standard 1st and 2nd class stamps you can avoid the wait by purchasing them in books of six or twelve at most newsagents or stamp vending machines.

In Eire the postal service is delivered by An Post and the sign to look out for is four wavy yellow lines preceding the word 'post' in white on a green background. Post Offices are usually painted a dark green colour.

The post in both the UK and Eire is reasonable.

In the UK there are two standards of mail delivery, first and second class. First class mail is targeted for next day delivery on the mainland, with second class deliveries being made the day after. Look for large, red cylindrical post boxes on pavements and street corners, or smaller red boxes set into walls and brickwork. International mail is variable, and depends largely on the delivery at the destination. For anything urgent you should use first class mail, but if the package is important then you should always use registered post.

In Eire there is only a single class of mail - at the moment - and internal mail is targeted for next day delivery, with European overseas deliveries within two to three days. Other destinations should be delivered within the week, depending on local services.

Telephones

Since the UK telephone service was opened to competition in the early 1980's, a number of service providers have appeared on the scene, and some have since vanished without trace. However the main operator in the public sector is still BT and they run the majority of public call boxes. Call boxes originally took coins, but more and more now take prepayment phone cards that can be purchased from newsagents and post offices. Some will take standard credit and debit cards, but you'll need to know your p.i.n. number in order to use them. However, away from the more populous areas coins are still mostly in use, with card/coin boxes beginning to appear in some places.

In Eire the primary telephone service provider is Eircom. Formerly known as Telecom Eireann, it was established in 1984 when it became semi-state owned. In May 2001 its mobile subsidiary Eircell, was sold to Vodafone.

To make an international call, dial 00 and when you get the tone, enter the country code followed by the area code and the number.

Useful country codes are:

34	Spain	32	Belgium
33	France	31	Netherlands
1	USA	49	Germany
353	Eire	41	Switzerland
39	Italy	351	Portugal
44	UK		

Scotland and Ireland have good coverage for mobile phone users. The four major network service providers are Vodafone, O_2 (formerly Cellnet), Orange, and T-Mobile (formerly One-2-One). All of them provide good reception in the cities and urban areas, but there are differences in the more rural areas. The current technology in use is GSM and most providers also offer a GPRS overlay service. If you're visiting from overseas, you should check with your service provider to see if they have a roaming agreement with a UK service provider, and make sure that you will be able to access the services you need along with any other arrangements that may be necessary. 3G mobile services are just starting to become available, but coverage at the moment is mostly restricted to the cities and major urban areas.

Documentation

In the UK there is no legal requirement to carry your vehicle and other personal documentation on you at all times. However, if you're stopped by a Police Officer or you're involved in an incident, you'll need to produce the appropriate documents at a Police Station within five days, so it's probably a good idea to have them with you, or at least back at where you're staying. And if you're visiting from abroad you should have your vehicle registration, insurance, and driver's licence documents with you as well as your passport. If you're travelling to Northern Ireland or Eire from the USA or Canada, then you'll also need to show your passport at the port of entry, but it's a good idea to have it with you anyway.

Insurance

If you're travelling to Scotland and Ireland from Europe or even further afield, then you should check with your insurance company or broker to ensure that your insurance meets the minimum British requirements. For peace of mind you'd be well advised to have fully comprehensive cover especially if you're carrying a pillion. Again, your insurance company or broker will be able to advise and arrange any short term extensions to your policy.

British insurance policies will give you the same cover in Northern Ireland that you have on the mainland, but you should check with your broker on the cover that you'll have as standard in Eire. Some policies will cover you for the whole of Ireland, but others may only give you basic cover once you go 'south of the border', and you could have to pay an additional premium to get the cover you need for the period of your stay.

Personal and Medical Cover

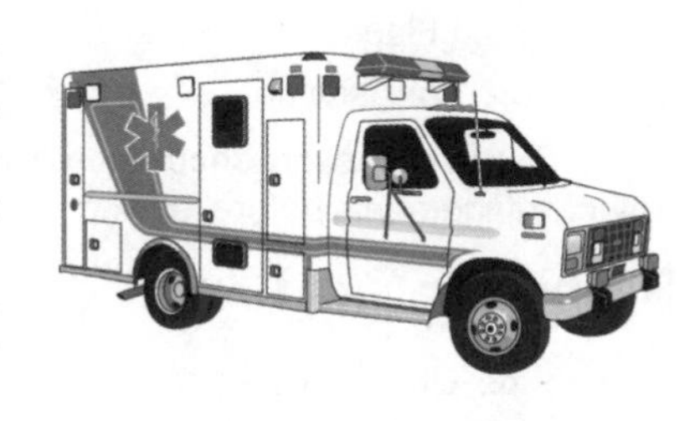

If you're a UK National and you're taken ill or suffer an injury while you're travelling around the country, then you can get medical attention under the National Health Service. Eire however, is a little bit different and should be treated as if it was a European Community country, which of course it is! This means that you'll need to have form E111 with you in order to benefit from the reciprocal health cover agreements that it has with other EC member states. But even with E111 to hand, the treatment that you'll receive could be fairly basic. You can obtain form E111 for free from your local Post Office, but do it before you leave. You'll need to fill in the personal details and get it stamped to get it validated.

However, with this basic medical care you'll still have to pay for any drugs that are prescribed, and if you need specialised treatment or even surgery, you could end up paying for that as well. If you're travelling to Eire you'd be well advised to take out additional personal travel and medical insurance that will cover all treatment that you need and will get you home as soon as possible, even to providing air ambulance facilities. There are a number of companies that provide this kind of cover, but make sure that whatever you choose it covers the use of motorcycles. The policies available from travel agents are geared towards package holidays and are usually not suitable. You'll also end up paying the travel agent's commission charges, which could be a significant sum. You can buy a short-term policy that will just cover the period of the trip, but if you plan on going abroad often, you'll find it cheaper to buy an annual policy. It's also possible to include medical cover with vehicle recovery.

Two useful sources for low-cost travel insurance that cater for motorcyclists are;

Matthew Gerard on 01483-730900

Direct Travel at www.direct-travel.co.uk

Vehicle Recovery

As well as taking out medical and accident insurance for yourself, you'd be well advised to take out cover for the bike as well. This will give you roadside assistance in case of a breakdown, get the parts to you that are needed for any repairs, and even get the bike back home when it's been damaged in an accident or if you're unable to ride it for whatever reason.

There are four major UK organisations offering both annual and short term cover. All these organisations also do travel insurance:

RAC European Motoring Assistance	08705-722 722	www.rac.co.uk
AA Five Star	0800-085 2840	www.theaa.com
Green Flag	0800-3288 772	www.greenflag.com
Europ Assistance	01444-442038	

Overseas visitors should contact their local motoring organisations for UK breakdown cover arrangements before leaving home.

Riding and the Law

In the UK and Eire traffic travels on the left-hand side of the road, unlike the other countries in the European Community.

If you're visiting the country for the first time and have never driven on the left before, this may seem a little daunting but it soon becomes automatic. It's certainly a lot easier on two wheels than on four. The first few road junctions you come to will need to be thought about carefully, as will roundabouts, so be cautious – it's better than being dead or in hospital. You'll soon feel that riding on the left is the most natural thing to do, but be careful in the early days after you've been riding a good distance on a great piece of road with no junctions – and then you come to a crossroads only to find that your brain has slipped back into 'home-mode'.

Don't forget to switch back to the other side of the road when you get home. It sounds obvious, but . . . . .

As far as the British and Irish law on using motorcycles on the road is concerned, it shares many points with other countries. Here are some of the more interesting features.

- Safety helmets must be worn at all times by both the rider and the pillion.
- Black visors are currently illegal in the UK, but can be used in Eire.
- Headlights do not need to be on when the bike is moving, but it's a good idea.
- The blood alcohol limit is 80mg. Make sure it's a lot, lot less.
- In Eire, the 'Give Way' sign is a red triangle, pointing downwards, with the words *Yield Right of Way* or *Geill sli*.
- In Eire, the Garda Siochana (Civic Guard) can issue a notice instructing a fine to be paid for a traffic offence. Normally this has to be paid within 21 days at a Garda Station, but they can also ask for on-the-spot payment if it's clear that you are only visiting the country for a short time.
- Speed limits in Scotland and throughout Ireland are:

Motorways and Dual Carriageways	**112 kph**	**70 mph**
Other roads outside built-up areas	**96 kph**	**60 mph**
Towns and built-up areas	**48 kph**	**30 mph**

Unless speed limit signs are specifically marked otherwise.

Maps and Information

The UK is perhaps one of the most comprehensively mapped countries in the world, and the maps produced by the Ordnance Survey are some of the best around. The 1:50,000 series covers the whole of the country in superb detail, but the complete set is a little too bulky to carry around in most tank bags. Other large scale maps are available, and a useful version is the Geographer's A-to-Z Handy Road Atlas, as it's small enough to fit in most map pockets and the scale is just big enough to read while on the move. Also worth looking at is the Tuffmap road atlas of GB & Eire that's also in A5 format, but is printed on a tear-resistant and waterproof synthetic paper called Yupo.

The Michelin 1:400,000 map of Ireland (sheet 712) is very useful, as is the Michelin map of Scotland (sheet 501). They are available from good bookshops like Waterstones and Blackwells, and larger branches of W.H. Smiths, as well as Stanfords in London and Bristol. Stanfords also provide an order and delivery service from their website at www.stanfords.co.uk.

If you plan on doing a bit of sightseeing while you're touring, then some good reads are the Rough Guide volumes for Scotland and Ireland (www.roughguides.co.uk). These are also available in a number of language translations.

Finally, some very much underrated sources of local information when you're touring the countryside are the local village stores, post offices and country pubs, especially in the more rural and out-of-the-way places. If you're in desperate need of some special service, or you want to find out more about some local feature, then these are good places to start asking questions.

Fuel

Unleaded petrol is available at all Scottish and Irish petrol stations. The pumps/nozzles are usually green and the fuel has a 95 octane rating. Look for an ultra low sulphur content fuel (ULS), as due to the complex workings of the British tax system this should be slightly cheaper. A Super Unleaded fuel is also widely available with a 98 octane rating. The old 4-star leaded petrol has now been superseded by the so-called 'lead replacement petrol' or LRP. This uses red pump handles and is often still marked with the four stars, which can be a little misleading. However it may disappear completely very soon as sales continue to fall.

It's still possible to get true leaded 4-star petrol, but the outlets are few and far between. Look for the name Bayford Thrust on the garage forecourt, or visit their website at www.leadedpetrol.co.uk to find the location of their outlets.

Diesel is also available at nearly every petrol station, and if you're visiting from the EU, then you'll be surprised at how expensive it is. But since there aren't any production bikes that run on diesel at the moment, this price difference is largely irrelevant. More to the point is the fact that diesel fuel pumps have either black or blue nozzles, so if you find yourself using one of these to fill your fuel tank, then you're probably just about to make a very expensive mistake!

Going Touring

So what's involved in going touring on your bike? I'm going to try and answer some if not all of your questions in this section. Everything here is based upon practical experience, sometimes by getting it wrong once and then working out the right way to do it, but also by seeing the results of other people's mistakes.

The Right Bike

The best bike to go touring on is the million-dollar motorbiking question, and you won't be surprised to discover that there's more than one answer. It all depends on who you ask.

Talk to a bike manufacturer or a dealer and it's got to be a fully-dressed tourer with panniers, top box, abs, cruise control, and all the bells and whistles that they can sell you. Very nice if you can afford it and if that's your thing, but for most of us the bike of choice is the one that we currently own; which means that you can go touring on just about anything - from a Pan European to a BSA Bantam - just so long as it's reasonably reliable and you're aware of its limitations. If you're taking a pillion then there's more things to consider, but I have seen people touring two-up on an R6 - that's either dedication or masochism, I'm not sure which! The truth of the matter is that having what someone else believes is the right bike is less important than you having the right frame of mind. I'd personally draw the line at a motocrosser or a stroker, but there are many who'd disagree, and even more who take classic or even vintage bikes on extended trips.

Planning the Trip

First of all you need to have some sort of idea of where you're going, what you're going to do when you get there, and for how long you're going to be away. It doesn't have to be incredibly detailed, but you need some sort of a plan. After all, you don't want to waste valuable time when you get there working out what to do next – you want to get on and do it! At the same time don't plan every hour of the trip, as this won't give you the flexibility to accommodate the unexpected, or to investigate something interesting that you may come across.

You could opt to head for a single destination, make that your base and ride out each day. Or maybe go for a full-blown tour with a new stop each night. Or something in-between. Think carefully about how many miles you can or will even want to ride each and every day. And don't forget to consider the capabilities of the bike that you're riding, and if you're travelling two-up then think about your pillion as well.

If there's a group of you going, do you all have the same riding ability? Having a couple of riders turning up at the hotel four hours after everyone else and just as they're serving the dessert, is not going to go down too well. And if it's your first time in that part of the country, be a little conservative about what you're trying to achieve. Allow time for refreshment and fuel stops and to take a look around. If you find you have time to spare each day, then you can always get out the maps and alter the routes. This is much better and less dangerous than riding 'til you're ready to drop at the end of each day.

CLOTHING

Once you've worked out where you're going, and for how long, you can start to think about how much clothing and other essentials you need to take with you. First of all there's the daily basics like socks, underwear, toiletries, T-shirts, etc. Then look at the weather you can expect at that time of year to determine warmth and waterproof factors of the other clothes that you'll need when you're not riding. The further north and west you travel in the UK the more likely you are to run into rain, although the British and Irish will tell you that you can expect rain any time and anywhere, it's a part of our heritage! More accurately, it's to do with the prevailing southwesterly Atlantic airstream. It's also going to get cooler as you head north. But don't forget that for most of the time you'll be wearing your bike clothing.

Finally, don't forget all those other essentials without which modern man (and woman) cannot survive – mobile phones/chargers, electronic organisers, personal stereo systems – you can make your own lists.

At the end of this exercise you'll probably find that you've assembled a small mountain of clothing and other items that you simply must take (if you have a pillion, it's a mountain range), and there's no way that it will all go on the bike. So what do you do?

- Pack the whole lot into a set of suitcases and go by car. Anyone who believes this is a serious option should stop reading this book immediately.
- Consider purchasing additional luggage for the bike. But if you've already fitted panniers, a top box and a tank bag, and your pillion wears a rucksack, then there's not a lot further you can go here - although a sidecar and a trailer could be an option for some!
- Pack as much as you can, and when you run out of new clothes halfway through the trip, you buy new stuff and throw the old clothes away. You could also get the chauffeur to deliver the luggage to the hotel each night in the Rolls Royce! Seriously though, if you're planning quite a long trip and your luggage and laundry facilities are limited, then this is a possibility especially for things like underwear and socks.
- Shorten the duration of the trip. What! – after you've done all the planning and made all the arrangements? You've got to be joking!
- Be ruthless with what you take. This really is the only option. Hotels, B&Bs and guesthouses are pretty relaxed in their dress standards, and jeans, T-shirt and trainers are not usually a problem; and if you're camping then you can wear what you please. Half a dozen T-shirts, a pair of jeans, another pair a lightweight trousers, shorts, a short-sleeved shirt, a sweatshirt and a fleece can keep you clothed for a couple of weeks with some careful management. You can also wash some 'small' items at overnight stops or find a laundromat in larger towns. Do you really need a complete change of clothes and shoes each evening – and a fresh shirt every day? And do you really want to turn your bike into a two-wheeled removals van? Remember, the object of the trip is to go touring on the bike – not to take part in a mobile fashion show!

But however ruthless you are, you'll nearly always find that you don't wear everything that you take. So you're still taking too much!

At the other extreme you could just take what you can get in your tank bag. However, after a few days travelling, you might find that some establishments refuse you admission!

If you're riding with a pillion, split the luggage capacity 50/50. Do not under any circumstances get into a discussion on this matter.

Finally, don't pack everything to capacity when you set out. Leave some space for those strange little knick-knacks that we all buy at some time or other when we're on holiday.

Other Essentials

As well as clothes, there are a number of other items that you should consider taking with you. Some of them also appear in other sections, but repetition is no bad way of getting a point across.

- Ear plugs. If you don't normally use them on the bike then you should. When you're riding long distances they're essential. Deafness from exposure to high noise levels is cumulative and non-reversible. That's the lecture over.
- Visor cleaning fluid/tissues. The country's flying insect population springs into life when the sun comes out and appears to be magnetically attracted to helmets. In summer your visor will need frequent cleaning.
- Waterproof winter gloves. It rains in Scotland and Ireland, even at the height of summer. Yes, really!
- Pocket knife/Swiss Army knife/Multi-tool. A thousand and one uses, too numerous to mention. You may never need it, but when you do you'll be glad you bought it with you. And it takes up so little space.
- Small torch such as a mini-Maglite. Useful for reading maps in the dark when you can't find the hotel or campsite at the end of a days ride, as well as looking for that essential item that's just fallen down inside the bike's fairing.
- First Aid kit for minor human body repairs to the cuts and grazes that we all seem to acquire on holiday. It should also have a supply of those little round white tablets that reconnect the body and mind to the environment after a heavy night discussing the day's riding!
- Spare light bulbs for the bike.
- Side stand pad. A small, durable plastic disk that's essential for sportsbike riders with no centre stand when you pull up on gravel parking areas. Why can you never find a flattened Coke can when you want one?
- Puncture repair kit. Obvious really, and much easier than carrying a spare.
- If you're coming to the UK from abroad then you must display a nationality sticker on the bike, or have a 'Euro' number plate fitted. Legally, any vehicle registered in one country that is used on the roads of another country, must display one or other of these at the rear of the vehicle.
- Cargo net. One of the best bike accessories ever invented. Increases the luggage capacity of any bike so that you can bring home those knick-knacks you've bought which won't fit in the panniers, because they're already full of clothes that you haven't worn. Also useful for carrying six-packs back from the supermarket.
- Spare set of bike keys. If you lose or damage your keys when you're a long way from home then you're really stuck. Unless you're very lucky and can get a spare cut locally, then the only alternative may be to have the bike recovered. End of holiday – game over! If you're travelling with a group of friends, swap the spare keys among

the group. Don't ever leave the spares on the bike, and if your bike has hard luggage then don't lock them in the panniers or top box! Sounds obvious, but it's been done before. If you're travelling with a pillion, then give them the spare set. Make sure you also have a spare transmitter for any alarm or immobiliser fitted to the bike, as well as a spare battery for same.

- A can of chain lube. You'll be riding a fair number of miles each day, and the chain and sprockets will get more than the usual amount of grief from the dust and water on the road. Do it religiously at the end of each day's ride and you shouldn't have any problems. Or fit an automatic chain oiler. Or buy a bike with shaft drive!
- A small roll of gaffer or tank tape. Invaluable for providing temporary fixes for a wide variety of motorcycle problems; from repairing cracked body panels, to securing damaged luggage, to holding zips together on clothing. Can also be used to protect the bike's paintwork from abrasion by soft luggage.
- Take along half a dozen cable ties as well and there's nothing you can't do a temporary fix on.
- If you've still got the warranty book for the bike, then there's a useful dealer list in the back that could help if you need emergency help or parts.
- A good disc lock, U-lock, or lightweight cable lock for that added piece of mind.

Luggage

Unless you're going to walk around in your riding clothes all day and every day and not change (Yeech!), you'll need some sort of luggage. Its capacity will really depend on how much you decide to take with you (see *Clothing*) and how long you're going for.

Luggage for motorbikes comes in two types – hard and soft. Which you choose to use will depend on personal preferences and also on the type of bike that you ride. But don't overload the bike. Any luggage that you fit will affect its handling, and the heavier it is and the further away from the bike's centre of gravity, the greater the effect. You can counteract this to some extent by winding up the pre-load on the rear suspension and perhaps stiffening the rear damping.

Check the bike's handbook for any advice from the manufacturer. When the bike's loaded up you'll also find that it's more susceptible to cross winds and air turbulence from other traffic. You may have to adjust your riding style, road speed and positioning to counteract these effects.

Hard Luggage

Considered by some to be the "Rolls Royce" option for touring, and by others to make a bike look like a delivery van, few would argue that hard luggage is eminently practical. Modern systems are made out of impact-resistant ABS plastics although one manufacturer uses aluminium, and are completely waterproof (Check the rubber seal between the lid and base before use, to make sure that it hasn't been damaged or started to rot – a light smear of Vaseline or similar can work wonders here). The cases attach to mounting frames that have to be fitted to the bike, but lock in place for added security when parking up for a break or going sightseeing. At the end of a day's riding they unlock quickly and easily, so that you can be showered, changed, and down in the bar while others are still fighting the bungee cords and buckles on their luggage. So if they're that good, why doesn't everyone use them?

- They're only available for certain bikes – the ones that are considered by manufacturers to be 'suitable' for touring.
- They're expensive – a full set of panniers, top box, and the fitting brackets is going to cost around £500-£600.
- The mounting brackets require some basic engineering skills to fit, but you could always pay your dealer to do this work for you.
- Purists will say that all the brackets and boxes spoil the bike's lines, although most systems these days are quite well styled.
- Top boxes are notorious for causing wind turbulence problems that affect a bike's handling. It's much reduced if you carry a pillion, in which case you'll probably need the extra luggage space anyway – and the pillion gets a backrest for free!
- If you change your bike, you'll need to buy and fit a new set of mounting brackets so you can re-use the cases - possibly.

At the end of the day the decision on whether to use hard luggage is a personal one, assuming that it's available for your bike. But if you're planning on doing some serious touring, then it's an option worth considering.

There's one final benefit of hard luggage that none of the manufacturers mention. If you're unfortunate enough to drop the bike, then panniers can prevent an awful lot of damage, both to the bodywork and the bike's mechanical components. Surprisingly, they'll probably only receive a few scuff marks or cracks at the worst, and a replacement will cost a lot less than a new fairing panel and engine covers!

Soft Luggage

This is the universal solution to carting stuff around on your bike. No matter what bike you've got, you should be able to find something to fit it.

Made from a heavyweight Cordura material, usually with a plastic inner coating, there's a variety of equipment available from a number of manufacturers over a range of prices. Generally speaking the more expensive the item, the better will be its build quality and the versatility of its fittings. However, it's always a good idea to take the bike with you when making a purchase, just to make sure that it will fit properly and not mask any of the controls. This is especially so for sportsbikes with high level exhausts. If you're using throwovers they must have plenty of clearance on the silencer(s), otherwise you could end up with a melted and burnt pair of jeans (seen that!)

Although some soft luggage claims to be waterproof, most isn't and will only keep the contents dry in a brief, light shower. Therefore unless you want to turn up in the bar at the end of the day looking as though you've just taken a shower with your clothes on, err on the side of caution and pack everything in waterproof bags before stowing them in the luggage. Heavy-duty plastic bin liners are ideal for this purpose. It's also a good idea to use a separate bag for each type of item that you're taking; T-shirts in one bag, underwear in another, etc., and label them accordingly. This way you don't have to unpack everything just to find a clean pair of socks.

There are four basic types of soft luggage; tank bags, pannier systems, tail packs and rucksacks.

Tank Bags. Considered by most people to be absolutely essential for touring. It should have a clear pocket on top for route instructions, notes, maps, etc., but if you're riding two-up and have a means of communicating with your pillion, you might want to think about using a back-mounted map pocket, and let them do the navigating.

Even if you've got hard luggage on the bike, you'll still find a tank bag useful. Most use magnets to attach the bag to the metal fuel tank, with an auxiliary strap that can be secured around the headstock. On most faired bikes, the magnets alone will hold the bag firmly in place at highly illegal speeds, but on un-faired bikes you'll need the strap as well to stop the bag hitting you in the chest at 90mph before disappearing down the road behind you! You might also want to consider putting a soft cloth or sheet of thin plastic over the tank to prevent the possibility of the bag scratching the paintwork.

If your bike has a plastic tank, then magnets are no good and you'll need a tank bag with a strap system to hold it in place. The French company Baglux do custom tank covers with clips to attach a variety of different shapes and sizes of bag. You can even have the whole lot colour-coded to match the bike's paintwork. Some bike manufacturers who use plastic fuel tanks (BMW, Triumph) produce their own tank bag systems. Talk to your dealer to find out what's available.

You should also check the height of the bag when you're sitting on the bike. Tourers have a more upright riding position and can accommodate a taller tank bag without obscuring the instruments or the road ahead. Sportsbikes by contrast, position the rider over the tank, and if the bag's too tall you may end up with the chin bar of your helmet resting on the top of the bag. If you've ever seen a rider peering over the top of a fully expanded tank bag on a 998 then you'll know what I mean.

Throwover Panniers. These fit over, under, or around the pillion seat of the bike, with a bag hanging down either side. They're held in place with a mixture of Velcro strips, plastic clips, and bungee cords, and offer a wide range of adjustment so that they'll fit almost any bike. There's one system that has a harness that you can leave on the bike, and then clip the bags to it when you want to carry luggage. Make sure that whatever system you choose fits your bike properly before parting with your money, or alternatively have the guarantee of a full refund if there's a fitting problem.

Check the following:

- They mustn't foul any part of the rear suspension at any point in its travel.
- They don't flap around in the breeze
- They can't be pulled off the bike in any direction, as you don't want them disappear-

ing down the road behind you. Be particularly brutal when checking this, but get a friend to hold on to the bike while you're doing it!

- They shouldn't obscure the pillion pegs or make it impossible to carry a passenger. You may be going solo on this trip, but next time it may be different!
- There should be at least one inch (25mm) of clear air between the panniers and any part of the exhaust system when stuffed full (most bags also have a heat reflective layer built into the lower face).

Different pannier systems have different capacities, but don't go straight for the biggest just on the grounds that it will give you more space. To make it fit properly and stay in place securely, soft luggage has to be filled. So if you're using it on a short trip, do you really want to have to fill half of it with newspaper or bits of foam rubber? Some systems offer a variable capacity by using zip-out expansion sections, so are worth considering.

And don't forget to protect any areas of the bike's bodywork that might be rubbed by the throwovers. A couple of strips of gaffer tape on the body panels can work wonders here.

Tail Packs. These used to be small bags that could be bungeed onto the pillion seat or rack, and were more suitable for weekend breaks, but I've also seen a leather suiter strapped to the back of a Fireblade! However, a number of manufacturers are now producing packs with capacities of around 60-90L, which is enough to keep most people supplied with life's essentials for a two-week trip. They come in a variety of designs from tubular sacks to things that look like expanding holdalls, with one type using a rack system that can carry one or two bags that zip together. Most of them use the pillion seat for the main support, which only makes them suitable for solo riders. However, some can be attached to a rack behind the seat, freeing up the pillion space, but you'll need to make sure that you don't overload the rack and its mountings.

Rucksacks. More personal luggage than bike luggage, and they're probably not the best choice for a touring holiday. If you're going to be away for any length of time then capacity is going to be a problem. You're going to need something like a 50-60L backpack, and doing 200+ miles a day with something that size on your back isn't going to be very comfortable or safe. You certainly won't be able to carry a pillion. A small day sack would be a much better proposition, but even something this size can cause pillion problems.

One item of personal luggage that is very useful on a bike is a "bum-bag". You can keep all your money and documents plus other oddments securely on your person at all times, but just make sure that it's got a locking buckle.

Bike Preparation

You've worked out where you're going to go, so you've got a reasonable idea of the mileage you expect to do, and you've got a feel for the load that you'll be carrying on the motorcycle. The next thing is to make sure that the bike will get you all the way there and back safely, in one piece, and without breaking down. This doesn't require an engineering degree, just a reasonable amount of common sense and a methodical approach. Of course, we're assuming before we start that the bike has been serviced regularly, is in good mechanical order, doesn't belch smoke from the exhaust and need a pint of oil every hundred miles, and the engine doesn't rattle like a bucket of nails.

First, it's a good idea to do a visual check on the bike. If everything looks OK and there's nothing about to drop off or fall apart, it's time to start our checklist.

1. When was the bike last serviced? Given the mileage that you expect to cover on the trip and the miles that you'll probably do before you go, will it be well past its next service interval before you get back? If so, then it's a good idea to pop it into your dealer for a good check over. Tell him what you're planning on doing and where you're going and he should be able to come up with a service scheme that will keep you going. Or you can always do the service yourself.
2. Check the condition of the tyres. Is there enough rubber on them to last the trip? If there's any doubt, fit new but keep the old covers. This is much less hassle than trying to get new tyres fitted while you're on your holiday. You can pop the old ones back on later and wear them down to the canvas when you're back home.
3. Give the bearings on the headraces, wheels and swing arm a good going over. Any play or binding should be investigated and corrected before you leave. You don't want the bike wobbling all over the place when you're negotiating a twisty B-road (unless you ride like that anyway!).
4. Check the brake pads and discs, front and rear. They're probably going to get a fair bit of punishment during the trip, so if the pads are more than half worn, get new ones and either fit them before you go or take them with you. Also check the operation of the brakes. If there's any sponginess they should be bled, and if the fluid's more than two years old it's probably a good idea to change it. Replacing the original rubber lines for braided Goodrich or Aeroquip type can rejuvenate your braking system.
5. Check all the control cables (throttle/choke/clutch) for smooth operation. If there's any notchiness or stiffness, then they probably need lubricating. This can be done with something like WD40, or better still use a cable oiler. If the problem persists, then the cable may be damaged and should be replaced before you go. Alternatively, take a spare cable which you could tape in place alongside the existing one to make it easier to fit.
6. Check the condition of the chain and sprockets. If there are any stiff links or the chain has passed its stretch limit or the sprockets are hooked, replace the lot.
7. Check the cooling system. If your bike is air or oil cooled then skip this. There should be no signs of any leaks and the rubber hoses should be in good condition. Any that show surface cracks when you pinch them should be replaced. Also make sure that all hose clips are tight. They can loosen over time as the rubber hose beneath them compresses and hardens.
8. Check the oil level and top up to Max if necessary.
9. Finally, make sure that all fasteners are secure and all the lights are working.

You might want to consider putting together a spares package to take with you. This could include such things as a small 1L can of engine oil, a spark plug, fuses, some electrical tape and any other small items that you consider useful.

And that's about it. The whole thing should only take you a couple of hours at the most.

Scotland On Two Wheels

For a lot of us 'English', a trip to Scotland involves a similar mileage as a trip to continental Europe. But as we can usually be assured of warmer (and drier) weather on the continent than we can get on our island home, it's not too surprising that a lot of us head across the Channel when we want to go bike touring. And that's a shame, because there's a wealth of excellent riding and spectacular scenery to be had without crossing any water.

Whilst it's true that Scotland will never be able to guarantee the kind of weather that you're likely to find in the south of France, it does have a lot of other things going for it; there's no real language problem - unless you're heading to certain parts of Glasgow! - currency, food and drink are all familiar items, and they drive on the same side of the road as the rest of the UK. This all adds up to shallow learning curve for a trip 'north of the border'. But there are a number of other things that you need to bear in mind.

The first is that Scotland is a popular tourist destination and has a limited road network that becomes more restricted the further north you go. This means that in the summer months there's a lot of traffic on the roads, and the geography means that the roads are narrow with few if any alternative routes between A and B. And when you mix the normal local traffic, which can be anything from private cars to 38-ton trucks, with the tourist influx, you get a sort of auto-governed 45 mph maximum speed, which is a bit annoying at times.

Second up is the famed Scottish midge, a small flying insect with a ferocious bite that appears in swarms in damp areas, particularly on the west coast. It's been said by some that the midge is the greatest deterrent to tourism in Scotland, so just think how busy the roads would be if someone could find a way of removing them completely !!

And finally there is the unreliability of the weather. Now the British are used to dodgy weather (some would say that they can't exist without it), but the mountains and glens of the Scottish Highlands in particular, can generate sudden changes in the weather and small micro-climates that can catch even the most experienced by surprise at times. You just need to make sure that you're prepared for as much as possible, particularly sudden and heavy showers.

So much for the cautionary tales. It may all sound a bit negative, but it's better to be aware of what may lie in store, rather than going in 'blind' and getting a few too many surprises - because there's no getting away from the fact that Scotland is a great place to visit on a motorbike.

Geography

As most of the traditional guide books will tell you, Scotland divides into three main geographical areas; the Southern Uplands of the Border Country, the Lowlands, and the Highlands which is where most of the tourists head for, and as a consequence where you'll find the most traffic and overcrowded roads. This isn't too surprising when you consider that this part of the country contains much of the most spectacular scenery; delivered through a combination of mountains, glens, rivers and lochs, surrounded by a rugged coastline and containing some of the few remaining wilderness areas in the UK. It's an inspiring landscape.

The Borders is an area that's frequently just passed through as people escape from

England and head north for the attractions of the Highlands, and that's a pity as it's a part of Scotland that has a lot going for it as a touring destination in its own right. While the scenery is nowhere near as dramatic as will be found further north, the rolling fells and the bleakness of the moorland landscape has a savage beauty all of its own. And the fact that most of the traffic is passing through on the main trunk roads and motorways, means that you'll find the really interesting roads almost deserted.

South of Kenmore

Between the two is the Lowlands, centred around the Firths of Clyde and Forth. This is the main population and commercial area of the country and is mostly visited for the attractions of Edinburgh and Glasgow. However, you don't have to stray too far north or south of the axis of these two cities to find good roads and interesting scenery. This is especially so to the north of Glasgow where a short twenty-mile journey will take you into the 'mini-highlands' of the Trossachs.

Geologically, the Highlands as we see them today are the result of erosive forces acting upon an ancient high plateau formed from rocks that date back as far as the pre-Devonian period. Most of this erosion has been caused by the simple forces of rain and wind, although in places the effects of glaciation are evident in U-shaped valleys. The area is separated into two distinct parts by the dislocation of the Great Glen that runs in a northeast/southwest direction. The land to the northwest of this fault line is generally at a higher level, and has a certain uniformity of features that is the result of both the geology of the region and the prevailing weather patterns. To the southwest of the fault the geology is more diverse, and that in turn produces a greater variety of scenery.

The Central Lowlands is a broad depression of much younger rocks, let down by parallel dislocations between the older rock masses to the south and the north. These dislocations have led to the formation of chains of high ground that are characterised by the hills of Fintry, Ochil, Renfrew, Sidlaw, Pentland and Campsie. Igneous rock intrusions are responsible for the spectacular crags and eminences that formed the foundations for the castles of Stirling and Edinburgh. Although the Lowlands only accounts for one-tenth of the country's area, it supports two-thirds of the population and this in turn gives a clue to the industrial and commercial importance of the region, long before the discovery of North Sea oil in the 1960s.

The Scottish Fells

This has its origins in the geology, which allowed easy communication and the exploitation of the coal, oil shales and iron ore deposits present in the carboniferous strata that underly this area.

Between the Lowlands and the English border, the Southern Uplands present a more rolling moorland landscape. In places, wide mossy moors, some 2,000 ft. or more above sea level and often as level as a racecourse, are broken up into flat-topped mountain plains by deep alluvial valleys. Around Tweedsmuir these smooth-topped green hills form excellent pasture land, while the valleys are given over to agriculture. Only on the higher ground can you find scenery reminiscent of the Highlands, where the weathering has formed gloomy corries, crags and talus slopes that are all the more spectacular when compared to the surrounding land. In Galloway to the southwest, the uplands have acquired a ruggedness unlike anything else in the area. This is a region where the underlying rocks have been pierced by intrusions of granite bosses, some of which have metamorphosed into crystalline schists.

Getting There

For the majority, taking a bike trip to Scotland means riding up through the north of England and then crossing the border. If you're travelling up the west side of the country, then the temptation is to get onto the A74(M)/M74 to get this part of the journey up to Glasgow over as quickly as possible.

Don't give into temptation, as when they built the motorway they left most of the old A74 virtually intact, but reclassified it as the B7076. This road is almost traffic-free, has an excellent surface, and parallels the motorway from Gretna to Abington. Use it from Lockerbie to Abington, and then take the A73 through Lanark and Airdrie to Kilsyth, to avoid the motorway traffic and delays around Glasgow. And don't forget that the Southern Uplands of Scotland has scenery to rival that of the more popular Highland area, but with much less traffic. So taking the less direct route has a lot of benefits if you're touring.

If you're heading up the east side of the country, then it's worth avoiding the A68 north of the Northumbrian border as it's absolutely littered with Gatso cameras; but if you can keep to the speed limits it's an excellent road. A better route would be to take the A1 as far as Scotch Corner, the A66 across the Pennines to Penrith, and the A6 to Carlisle. Use the M6 to bypass the town and then the A74(M) to Lockerbie.

From Northern Ireland, you'll arrive in Stranraer from where you can take the excellent A77 coast road up to Ayr, where it strikes inland through Kilmarnock to pick up the motorway 'ring road' around Glasgow.

What to See

There's so much to see in Scotland that it's difficult to know where to start. In the Central Lowlands there is a plethora of sights in Glasgow and Edinburgh, and any good guide book will give you all the details that you could need.

To the south of this main conurbation, the Borders is an area of contrasts. In the west the Southern Uplands is a mixture of round-topped hills and bleak moorland, split by narrow glens, fast-flowing rivers and black water lochs. To the west the Tweed valley has a green lushness about it that is in sharp contrast to the moorlands of the Cheviot hills that divide

Scotland from England. If you're in to ruined abbeys, castles and keeps, then there's an amazing number to choose from in the Borders. This was an area that suffered from endless clan warfare not to mention both English and Scottish raids during medieval times. The general unrest and instability of the region is reflected in the ruins that are scattered across the landscape.

In the Highlands, the scenery is the main attraction and there's so much of it that the brain almost goes into overload. Although the spectacular Glen Coe seems to be high on most people's list, once you get up into the mountains almost everything is worth seeing. If you're into a 'wee tipple', then it will be difficult to miss out on a visit to Speyside and a tour around one of the distilleries. But take away a miniature rather than have a tasting! Further north, and you'll be getting into some of the remotest areas in the country, the roads are few and far between and many are only single-track. This is really serious walking territory. Beyond this there's the islands of Orkney and the Shetlands for the true long distance traveller.

On the east coast, the Isle of Skye acts like a magnet for many people, with the Cuillin and the Red Hills providing a dramatic backdrop to the rugged coastline. Other islands offer other attractions, not least Islay with its solitude and distilleries which produce a spirit with a characteristic peaty quality. But be aware of two things; this is one of the wettest parts of the country, and if you're planning on doing a lot of island hopping then you'll need to make allowances for the cost and the time taken for the ferry crossings.

Accommodation and Information

The one good thing about Scotland is that there is no shortage of places to stay, no matter what your budget. With a range from campsites to four-star hotels, it's not too difficult to find something suitable, but if you want to get out into the countryside then you'll be better off looking at the large range of self-catering and bed & breakfast accommodation.

A good place to start is the Scottish Tourist Board. They can be contacted on +44 (0)131-332 2433 or through the internet at www.visitscotland.com. They are the main tourist agency for the whole of Scotland, but within the organisation are a number of local tourist boards.

Accommodation Scottish Style

All of the tourist boards listed in the following table provide an accommodation booking service and can also post area and accommodation guides to your home address.

Tourist Board/Information	Website Address
Angus & Dundee Tourist Board	www.angusanddundee.co.uk
Argyll, the Isles, Stirling, Loch Lomond & the Trossachs	www.scottish.heartlands.org
Ayrshire & Arran Tourist Board	www.ayrshire-arran.com
Dumfries & Galloway Tourist Board	www.galloway.co.uk
Edinburgh & Lothians Tourist Board	www.edinburgh.org
Grampian Highlands, Aberdeen & the North East Coast	www. castlesandwhisky.com
Greater Glasgow & Clyde Valley Tourist Board	www.seeglasgow.com
The Highlands of Scotland Tourist Board	www.host.co.uk
Kingdom of Fife Tourist Board	www.standrews.com/fife/fifehome.htm
Orkney Tourist Board	www.visitorkney.com
Perthshire Tourist Board	www.perthshire.co.uk
Scottish Borders Tourist Board	www.scot-borders.co.uk
Shetland Islands Tourist Board	www.visitshetland.com
Scottish Tourist Board	www.visitscotland.com
Western Islands Tourist Board	www.witb.co.uk

Campsites in Scotland and Ireland have long been a poor relation of their continental cousins, but things are slowly improving. Whilst there are still site owners whose idea of a suitable pitch is the corner of a ploughed field with a standpipe half a mile away outside the chemical toilet hut, these places are gradually dying out - probably due to cholera, typhoid, dysentery, etc!

As well as the references in the list above, the following books are useful guides to campsites and camping in Scotland and Ireland as well as the other countries in the UK, and can be obtained from most good bookshops.

Title	Publisher	
Alan Rogers' Good Camps Guide: Britain and Ireland	Haynes Publishing	Quality campsites and caravan parks all individually inspected. Lists over 400 sites which are inspected and reviewed regularly. It also has information such as parks for adults only, boat launching, camping for people with disabilities and much more.
Camping and Caravan Parks in Britain	English Tourism Counci	The Official guide from the English Tourism Council. Quality assessed camping accommodation in Britain. The listing is in English but instructions on how to use it and useful information are given also in German, Dutch, French and Italian.
AA Caravan and Camping: Britain & Ireland	AA Publishing	Over 1000 sites inspected and given AA pennant ratings. An up-to-date guide to camping establishments in Great Britain and Ireland by the AA. Every campsite is described and graded, contact numbers and websites where available. Photos are given of many establishments.
Camping Sites	IPC Magazines	Top quality sites for tents and motorhomes across the UK. Lists hundreds of sites in England, Wales, Scotland, Northern Ireland and Southern Ireland. Most entries have a star grading, and all include details of location and facilities available.

Roads and Routes

There's lots of good biking roads in Scotland, although like most places the further you get from the major population areas, the better the riding experience. Fortunately for us, most of the population is concentrated in the Lowlands around Glasgow and Edinburgh, so once you're clear of these commercial centres there's plenty of choice.

But just remember that the rugged countryside means there are few roads, and these attract a lot of tourist traffic in the summer months. And don't think that the powers-that-be don't know where the good biking roads are as well. Unfortunately they've recently been well publicised by the irresponsible antics of a few, and as a result there's a significant police presence on many roads at summer weekends.

Anyway, here are a few ideas based upon personal experience, and I'm sure that you'll find lots of others.

The Falls of Dochart

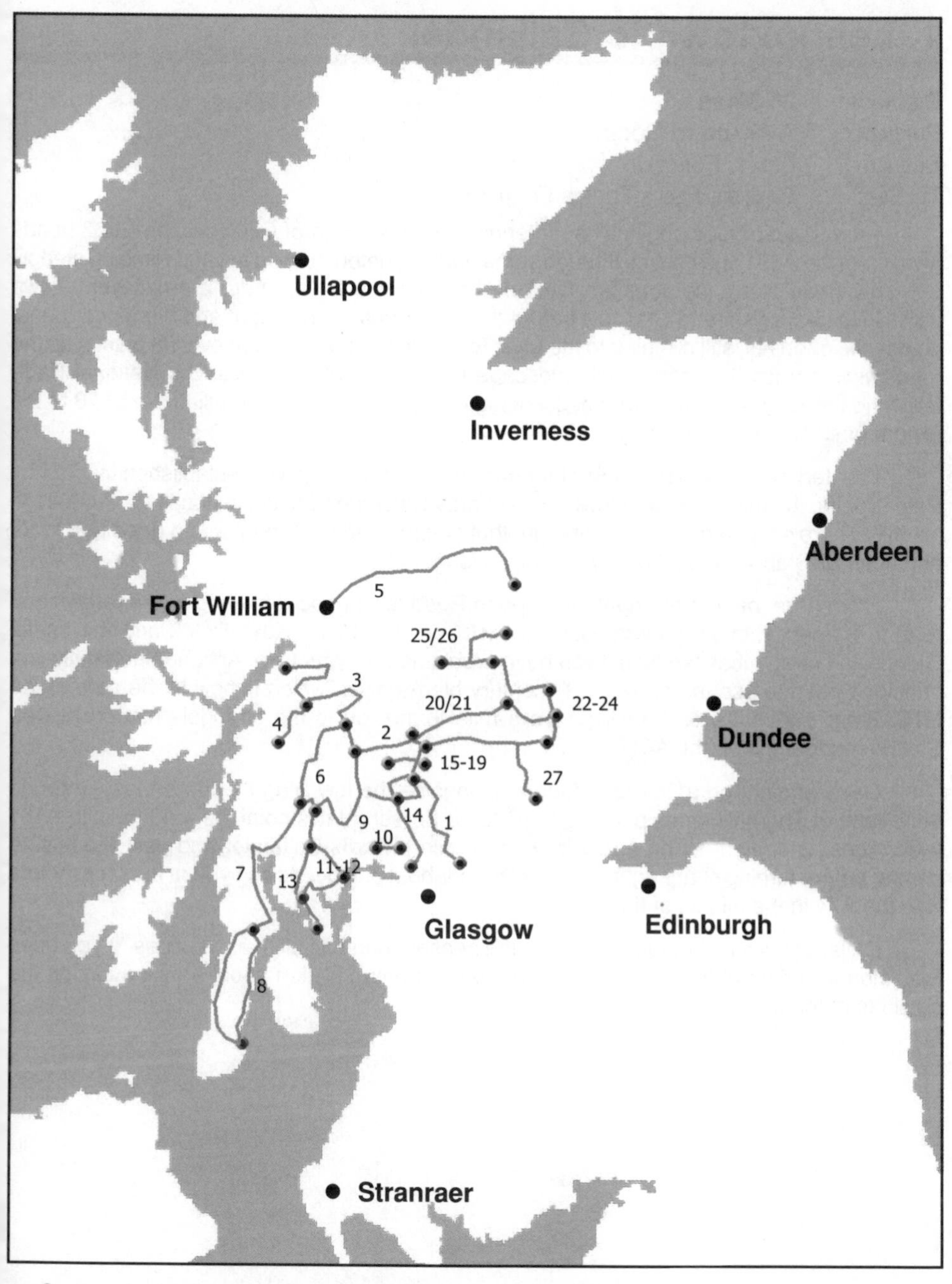

Scotland showing approximate locations of major towns and the routes in this guide

1. Lennoxtown to Callander

Distance: **25 Miles**
Surface: **Average to Good**
Scenery: **Fells, Forestry**
To See: **Campsie Fells,Torrie Forrest**

From inauspicious beginnings in Lennoxtown just north of Glasgow, the B822 heads away from the A891 and passes through some housing before turning left and climbing steeply up Crow Road along the southern flank of the Campsie Fells. There are excellent views across Dumbartonshire to Glasgow before the road turns sharply right and heads northeast across the open fell, still climbing to the Muir Toll. The surface is a bit uneven in places as the road twists across the remote fell landscape of this part of the Trossachs National Park, following the River Carron, before descending in a gradual arc and crossing the B818 to the picture postcard village of Fintry.

Located at the head of the Strathendrick valley, the village was established in 1794 by Peter Speirs, the mill owner and resident of nearby Culcreuch Castle, to house the workers in his mill. There's a pub here, the Fintry Inn, that can provide refreshment and good pub food, and even B&B accommodation if you fancy a longer stay.

From here, bear to the right into Kippen Road for a good run along a hedgerow-lined road to Kippen, with it's general store, the 18th century Cross Keys Hotel, and the useful Glengoyle Garage that can help if you have problems with your bike. Although hopefully you shouldn't need to use the original 18th century blacksmiths, which is now in the care of the NTS. From the centre of the village it's a mile further on to the strangely named Kippen Station roundabout on the A811.

Carry straight on at the roundabout, alongside the low-lying Flanders Moss, through the village of Thornhill, and up through the Torrie Forest. At this point the road joins the A81 which runs as straight as an arrow for over a mile towards Callander and past the leisure centre, before turning sharp right at a small roundabout and depositing you at the cross roads with the A74 in the middle of the town.

Callander is a busy tourist centre in the season, and has all main services. If you need fuel, then turn right at the traffic lights and there's a petrol station about a mile away on the outskirts of the town.

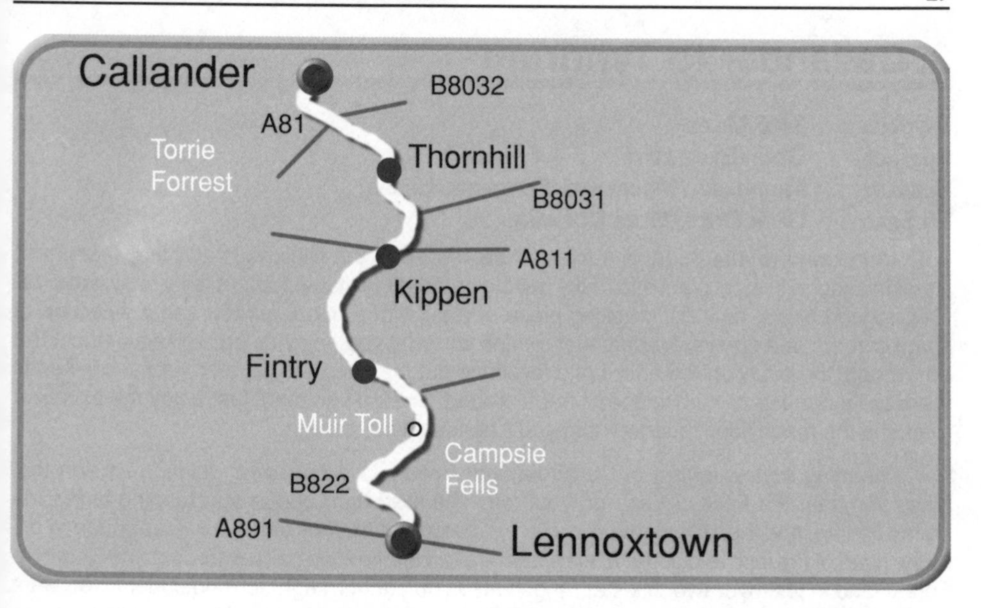

Road	Direction	Comment
B822	Fintry	Follow the southern flank of the Campsie Fells and on up to Muir Toll
B822	Kippen	Bear right at Fintry into Kippen Road and follow the B822 to Kippen
B822	Thornhill Callander	Straight on at the roundabout where the B822 crosses the A811 towards Thornhill
A81	Callander	Straight on where the B822 joins the A81 to Callander
A81	Callander	Right at the roundabout to the town centre. For fuel turn right at the lights - its about a mile

2. Callander to Tyndrum

Distance: 34.5 Miles
Surface: Good/Excellent
Scenery: Mountains, Moorland, Forestry, Lochs
To See: Glen Ogle, Glen Dochart

Although the A84/85/82 is a major trunk route into the Highlands and the west coast, it's wide enough in most places to make getting past the inevitable traffic a fairly easy exercise. This is good news, as it's a cracking piece of road with a good surface and a selection of sharp corners and open sweepers that remind you why you enjoy riding a bike so much! But be warned; the crazy speed antics of a few have put the police on full alert and at weekends there are a number of mobile speed traps around. So don't go mad, just enjoy the excellent road and the magnificent scenery that you'll be travelling through.

Heading northwest out of Callander, you head into a narrow undulating section that takes you past the Falls of Leny on your left. The road then opens out, running alongside Loch Lubnaig, and then through a series of quick corners that will stop your tyres squaring off. At the head of the loch and some 8 miles from Callander the road passes through the Strathyre Forest, and in just over two miles at Kingshouse you can turn right to Balquidder if you want to see Rob Roy's grave in the small churchyard (see also Route 19). After 13-odd miles the road enters Lochearnhead where you turn left onto the A85, right leads towards Crieff and Route 18.

The route now climbs up the east flank of Glen Ogle through a narrow section that often generates queues of crawling vehicles. If you're stuck in a queue at the bottom of the pass, be patient as it will be a lot easier (and safer) to work your way around the traffic as the road climbs, straightens, and the visibility improves. Grab a look across the valley to your right if you've got a moment, and you'll see the remains of the old railway viaduct that once took the trains through to Crianlarich. Once over the pass, the road descends through a number of sweeping turns, some of which are a little tighter than you may think at first sight. There are frequent accidents on this stretch of road as the debris on the road verges will testify.

After 20 miles you'll reach the bottom of the pass where the A827 branches off to the right to take you to Killin (2 miles - useful shops, good accommodation, and refreshments see Route 20), the Falls of Dochart, Loch Tay and Aberfeldy. Just past this is the Lix Toll garage where you can get fuel and mechanical assistance if needed.

The road descends a little further through a twisty wooded section before it reaches the bottom of Glen Dochart. At this point the road opens out and runs along the south side of the valley. If the sun's out, then there's some magnificent views along here. There's not a lot to see or do in Crianlarich, so carry straight on, following the signposts to Fort William and taking the sharp left and right under the railway bridge. If the road's wet here, then take care over the manhole covers that are conveniently placed right on the normal line on both sides of the bridge.

The next five miles of the A82 are not particularly exciting, but at 34½ miles in Tyndrum there's a Little Chef on the left and the strangely named Green Welly Stop on the opposite side of the road where you can also get refreshments, refuel at the Shell garage, and buy a pair of the green rubber boots if you're that way inclined.

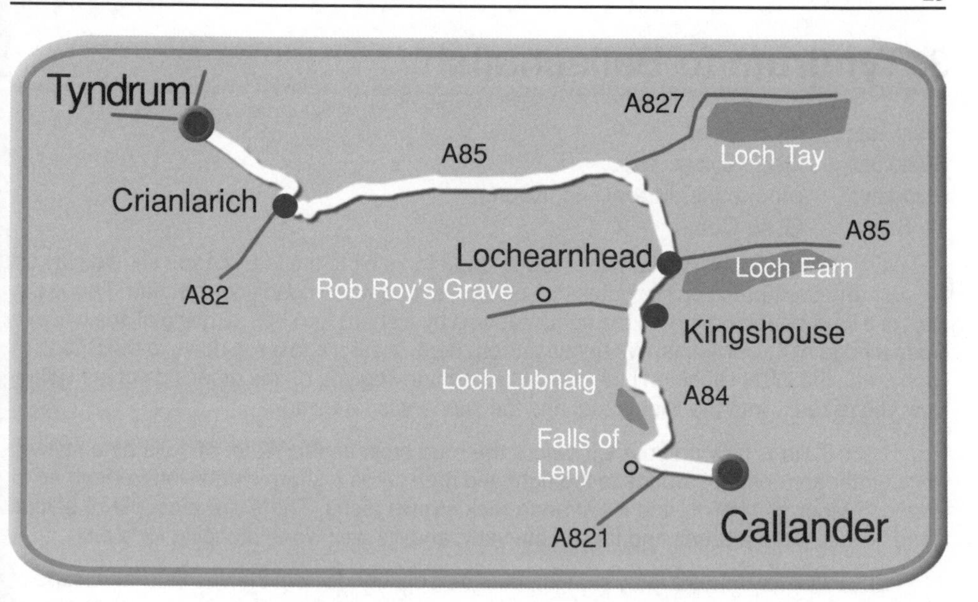

Road	Direction	Comment
A84	Lochearnhead	Head west from Callander, with the Falls of Leny on your left, to Kingshouse
A84	Lochearnhead	At Kingshouse turn right and back under the main road to Balquhidder to see Rob Roy's grave or continue on the A84
A85	Crianlarich	Turn left onto the A85 and over the Glen Ogle. Turn right onto the A827 for the falls of Dochart and Loch Tay before continuing on to Crianlarich
A85	Fort William Tyndrum	Sharp left and right under the bridge out of Crianlarich and follow signs for Fort William and Tyndrum *(then carry straight on for Route 3)*

3. Tyndrum to Ballachulish

Distance: **46.5 Miles**
Surface: **Good/Excellent**
Scenery: **Mountains, Moorland, Lochs**
To See: **Glen Coe,**

On the way out of Tyndrum the A85 to Oban forks off to the left, but you should stay on the A82 and pass between the gates that close the road when conditions get bad. This is the start of a long sweeping turn to the right, followed by a sharp turn left, climbing all the while to cross a ridge of the Grampian Mountains. From here, there's a fast run down to the Bridge of Orchy, with the West Highland Line railway accompanying you on the other side of the valley. Now you're really into the Highlands, and the scenery is fantastic.

Loch Tulla is now on your left before the road crosses the Water of Tulla by a striking white girder arch bridge, swings to the right and then takes a sharp hairpin left to climb up to Rannoch Moor at 1181 ft. and it's strange rock-strewn lochs. There are a couple of places along here to have a break and take in the view, and it's well worth stopping for a bit.

The road now takes a fairly straight route as it descends from the desolate landscape of the moor and heads straight into the spectacular valley of Glen Coe over another one of those white girder arch bridges. The road runs along the right-hand side of the wide glacial valley floor, beginning a gradual climb up into the confines of the glen itself. Halfway down on the left there's a popular parking area with some great views.

After the splendour of the glen, the village of Glencoe at 30 miles, is a bit of a disappointment. However, you should turn right here and take the B863 to Kinlochleven. This used to be the main road to Fort William before the ferry across the mouth of Loch Leven was replaced by the bridge that now joins North and South Ballachulish. It's wide, well-surfaced, and goes up and down and twists and turns like a demented dervish. It's also deserted!

At the head of the loch, take a break in one of the pubs and hotels in Kinlochleven, before running back down the north side of the loch along another set of twists and turns to North Ballachulish. At the T-junction you can turn right and head up to Fort William, or go left and cross the bridge back to Glencoe.

Climbing onto Rannoch Moor

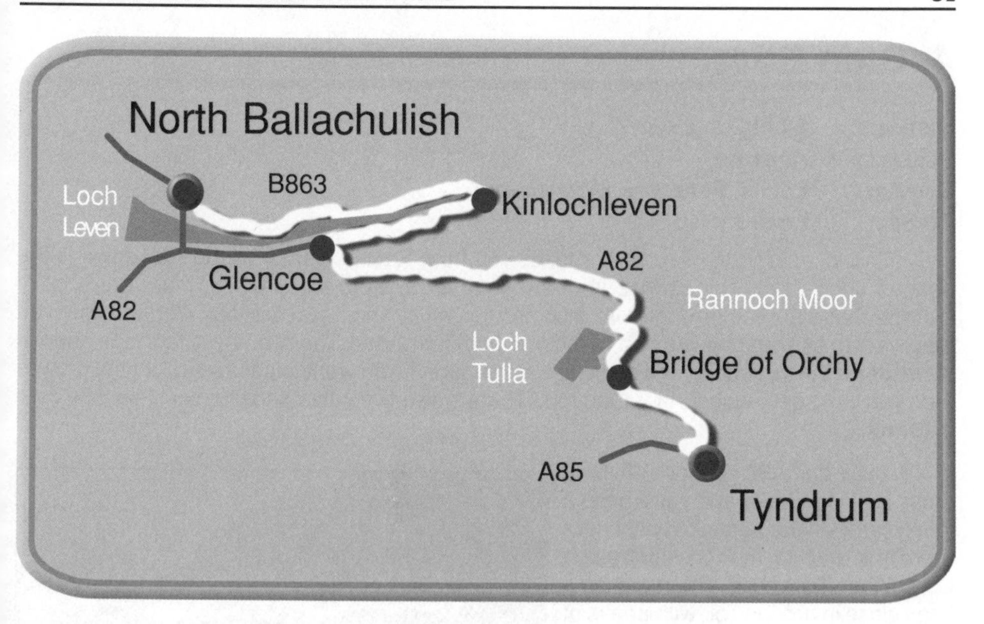

Road	Direction	Comment
A82	Fort William	Leave Tyndrum on the A82 and stay on the A82 as the A85 to Oban forks off to the left
A82	Fort William	Loch Tulla on the left. Stay on the A82 over Rannoch Moor all the way to Glencoe
B863	Kinlochleven	Turn right at Glencoe onto the B863 and follow the road around Loch Leven to North Ballachulish. Turn right here to continue to Fort William or left to go back to Glencoe across the bridge

4. Glen Etive

DISTANCE: **14 MILES (EACH WAY)**
SURFACE: **AVERAGE**
SCENERY: **LOCHS, FORESTRY, MOUNTAINS**
TO SEE: **LOCH ETIVE**

This is a single track road that takes you from Rannoch Moor all the way down to the head of Loch Etive. The surface is pretty good for most of the way, but there are a lot of surface changes over its length. It's also narrow, twisty and if you manage 40 mph, then you may want to stop and have a rest to recover from the shock! The scenery is fantastic and the views down the loch at the end of the trip are superb. If you want to get away from the crowds then you can't get much further than this! There's also five cattle grids to cross, so take care if it's wet.

Take the A82 to Fort William, cross Rannoch Moor and you'll pass a lonely hotel on the right. Just past here there's a road to the left signposted Loch Etive. Turn here. The mountains soon close in around you with peaks of over 3,000 ft. as the road follows the course of the river that drains off the moor. The Royal Forest is on your right as the road rises and falls, clinging to the side of the hill and following the ever narrowing valley before curving to the right around Buachaille Etive Moor and dropping into the wide valley at the small hamlet of Dalness. The road now runs along the valley floor, crossing numerous side streams that drain off the hills, and a loch that's almost completely enclosed by the mountains.

GLEN ETIVE

At Invercharnan the road climbs up into forestry, and you should keep an eye open for the local wildlife here. I came round a corner and found a full-grown stag in the middle of the road, not more than 30 ft. away! The road keeps on twisting and turning, rising and falling, and then crosses a narrow bridge before dropping down to the side of Loch Etive. There's a cottage and smallholding here, and most of the animals seem to live in the middle of the tarmac! The short run alongside the head of the loch finishes in a gravel area beside a wooden jetty that's definitely seen better days. From here there are marvellous views down the loch and across to the summit of Stob Cair an Albannaich at 3,425 ft. This is a lonely and desolate spot, but the scenery is outstanding. Now you can turn around and ride all the way back.

LOCH ETIVE LOOKING TOWRADS THE SEA

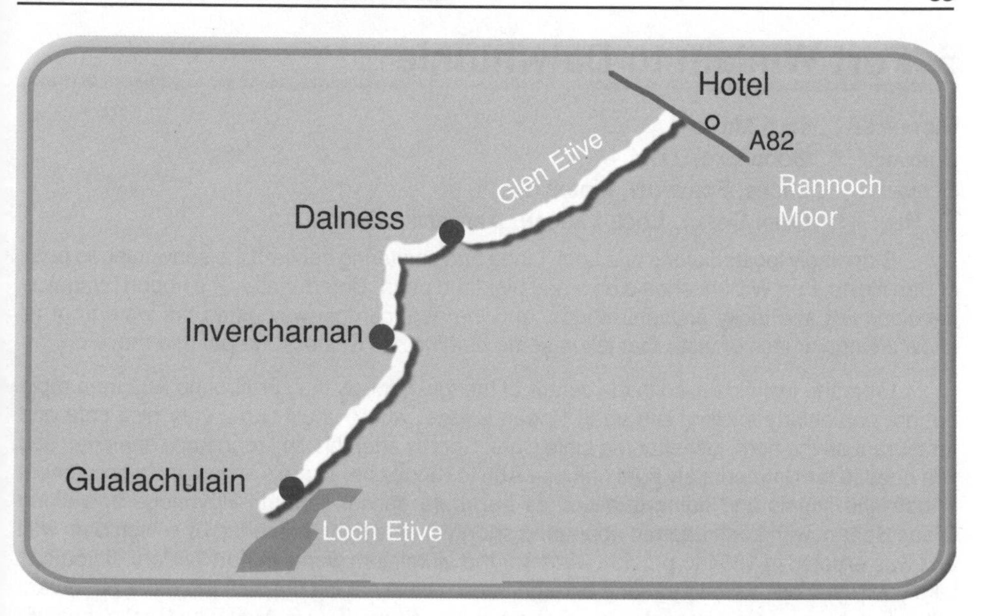

Road	Direction	Comment
A82	Fort William	At the hotel just past Rannoch Moor turn left
Unmarked	Loch Etive	Follow the road down Glen Etive to the Loch. Beware of the local wildlife but the views are spectacular. Once you have reached the end of the road there is no other way out than back the way you came!

5. Fort William to Dalwhinnie

DISTANCE: **45.5 MILES**
SURFACE: **GOOD/EXCELLENT**
SCENERY: **LOCHS, FORESTRY, MOUNTAINS**
TO SEE: **GLEN SPEAN, LOCH LAGGAN, ARDVERIKE CASTLE**

Stunningly located alongside Loch Linhe and sheltering beneath the snow capped peak of Ben Nevis, Fort William should be a real highland pearl. Unfortunately the ribbon bungalow development, the tacky souvenir shops, and the dual carriageway along the waterfront all show a singular lack of taste that takes some beating. So re-stock, re-fuel and move on.

From the lochside road in the centre of the town, follow the northbound A82 for a rapid but not particularly exciting run up to Spean Bridge, where you'll find a very nice cafe and restaurant on the right, just after the Little Chef. Shortly after this, the road turns sharp left and you need to turn immediately right onto the A86 to Kingussie. There's an instant improvement in both the scenic and riding qualities as the route passes through Roybridge and along Glean Spean, with Loch Laggan appearing shortly on the right, preceded by a high dam wall that was erected in 1934 to provide water for the aluminium works in Fort William. If you can take your eyes off the road for long enough, then halfway along the loch the more observant will notice an extremely imposing building on the far shore. This is Ardverike Castle, and will be instantly recognised by fans of the BBC TV series *Monarch of the Glen*. The good riding and the scenery continues past the end of the loch, although the land begins to flatten off as you head east. Some 37 miles from Fort William the road turns sharply left, and immediately after this at Drumgask you need to turn right onto the A889 to Dalwhinnie. After a few hundred yards there's a pottery on the left, with an extremely appealing cafe, not least for the selection of fresh home-baked cakes and scones that are on offer. And if you eat too much and simply can't go any further, there's a bunkhouse round the back where you could possibly sleep off your gluttony.

Those less corpulently challenged, should remount and continue on the A889, climbing gently out of the Spey Valley, through Catlodge to the village of Dalwhinnie some 8 miles further down the road. As you enter the village the distillery's on the left, and a short distance further on ther is just a petrol station-cum-general store opposite a large lodge-type building - the Loch Erich Hotel. This is a very open and windswept area and it must be particularly bleak and uninviting in the middle of winter.

THE SPEY VALLEY

About a mile further down the road, the A889 joins the A9 at a T-junction. Turn left for Aviemore, Inverness and beyond, turn right for Pitlochry and the south.

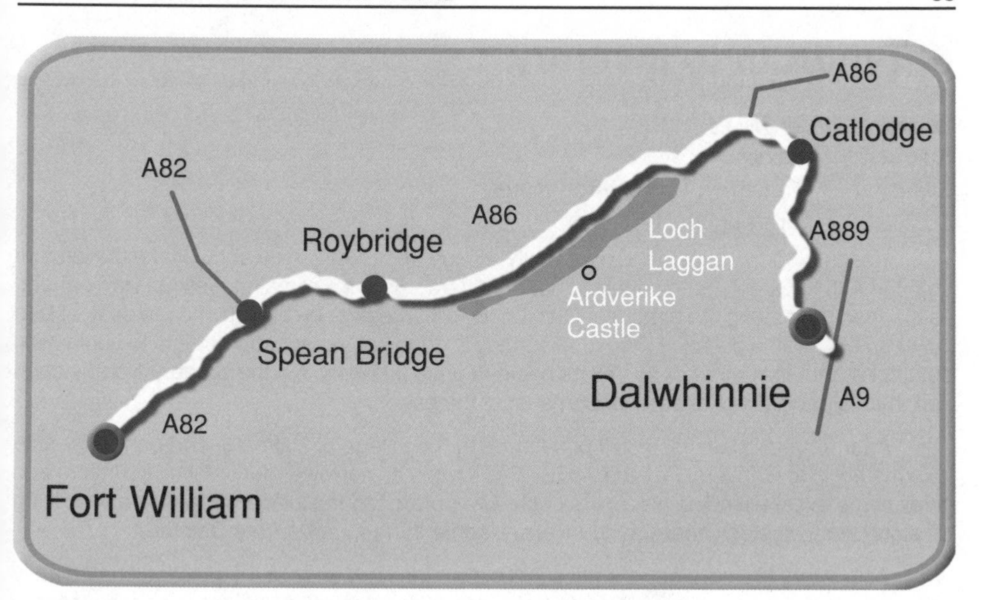

Road	Direction	Comment
A82	Spean Bridge	Follow the A82 north out of Fort William
A86	Kingussie	Turn right onto the A86 immediately after a sharp left at Spean Bridge
A86	Kingussie	Ardverike Castle on your right across Loch Laggan
A889	Dalwhinnie	Turn right onto the A889, cafe on the left after about 100 yards
A889	Dalwhinnie	Distillery on your left. Join the A9 just outside Dalwhinnie. Turn left for Aviemore and right for Pitlochry

6. Tyndrum to Inverary

Distance: **27 Miles**
Surface: **Good**
Scenery: **Forestry, Lochs, Mountains**
To See: **Glen Lochy, Inverary**

Heading north out of the 'Green Welly' village on the A82, you should take the left fork onto the A85 to Oban after a couple of hundred yards. There's some marvellous views ahead as the road runs along the bottom of Glen Lochy with the river on the left and the peak of Ben Lui at 3,706 ft. in the distance. The road surface is good and reasonably straight to begin with, but after a about six miles or so, things begin to get a bit twisty, but the scenery's pretty open and there's good views ahead through a lot of the bends.

After another six miles you'll pass through the village of Dalmally, and on the far side take the left turn to Inverary on the A819. This road is bit narrower but still well surfaced, and gives some excellent riding alongside Loch Awe before turning inland at Cladich and striking off along the forrested Glen Aray to Inverary, some thirteen miles from Dalmally.

At Inverary there's a petrol station just before the road ends at a T-junction immediately after passing under an arch. Turn right here along the edge of Loch Fyne, and then left into the parking area where the main road swings round to the right. Parking is very tight here, but if you continue round the end there's usually space to squeeze a couple of bikes in, just opposite the useful cafe.

The town of Inverary dates only from the 18th century, being built by the Duke of Argyll as a 'new town' on the site of a derelict fishing village so that he could establish a commercial centre for the region. Its classic Scots-Georgian architecture, with its whitewashed walls and window casements picked out in black makes it very photogenic, which accounts for it's popularity with the tourists.

Loch Fynne

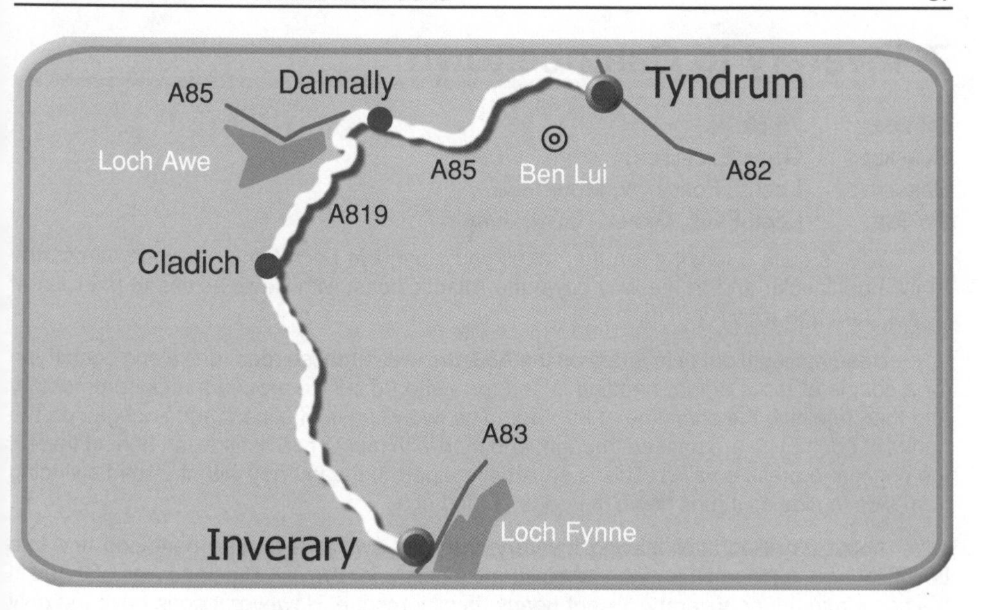

Road	Direction	Comment
A82	Fort William	Just outside Tyndrum take the left fork for the A85 and Oban
A85	Oban	After 6 miles you come to Dalmally. Turn left here onto the A819 to Inverary
A819	Inverary	Follow the A819 all the way to Inverary. Petrol station at Inverary just before the arch.
		Turn right where the A819 meets the A83 and follow the road along Loch Fynne. Parking is on the left in the car park

7. Inverary to Campbeltown

DISTANCE: **75 MILES**
SURFACE: **GOOD/EXCELLENT**
SCENERY: **LOCHS, FORESTRY, MOUNTAINS**
TO SEE: **LOCH FYNE, GIGHA, ISLAY, JURA**

This is quite a lengthy run that takes you alongside Loch Fyne and then across the Kintyre peninsular and all the way down the Atlantic coast with views across to the isles of Gigha, Jura and Islay.

Heading south out of Inverary on the A83, the well-surfaced road runs along Loch Fyne for a couple of miles before heading inland for a short distance around a rocky promontory and then rejoining the shoreline at Furnace. The two villages of Minard and Lochgair on the banks of Loch Fyne are passed through, and then with most of civilisation left behind there's the chance to press on a bit. This is an excellent part of the journey with the road swinging from side to side as it runs down the edge of the Loch.

About 23 miles after leaving Inverary, the road swings around a headland and into Lochgilphead. Although this is the administrative centre for Argyll & Bute and was planned in the same manner as Inverary, it's not nearly as picturesque. However it does have the only bank and supermarket for miles, and even boasts a swimming pool.

Turn left here at the roundabout, where there's a useful petrol station, go straight on at the next roundabout in the town centre and then left at the third roundabout as the A83 runs around the head of the small Loch Gilp from which the town takes its name. The road runs between Loch Fyne and the Crinan Canal, and then a couple of miles further on it crosses the entrance to the canal at Ardrishaig. The lochside run continues for another 11 miles of fun, with some excellent twists and turns and views across the loch to Argyll and Bute before dropping down into Tarbet, where there's another petrol station on the right. In Tarbet the A83 turns sharp right to cross the promontory and then West Loch Tarbet appears on the right. At Kennacraig there's a small terminal on the right for ferries to Islay and Jura and the single track road to Campbeltown heads off to the left.

After a short excursion inland, the road rejoins the coast and both the tarmac and the view opens out as the road goes through the village of Ballochroy. From here there's a wonderful 20 mile run down to Campbeltown with the Atlantic and the Isles keeping you company on the right. It's usually quite breezy here even on the calmest days, but if the wind's up then take care as it will really blast across the road.

CAMPBELLTOWN HARBOUR

When you get to Campbeltown, go straight into the town, following the road round to the left and down the High Street to the roundabout by the side of Loch Fyne, where there's easy parking on the harbour pier by the tourist information office. Campbeltown is not a major tourist destination, in fact it looks a little rundown and tired, but is has all the services you could need including a small supermarket (head north on the B842 to Carradale, turn right at the T-junction, and it's on the left).

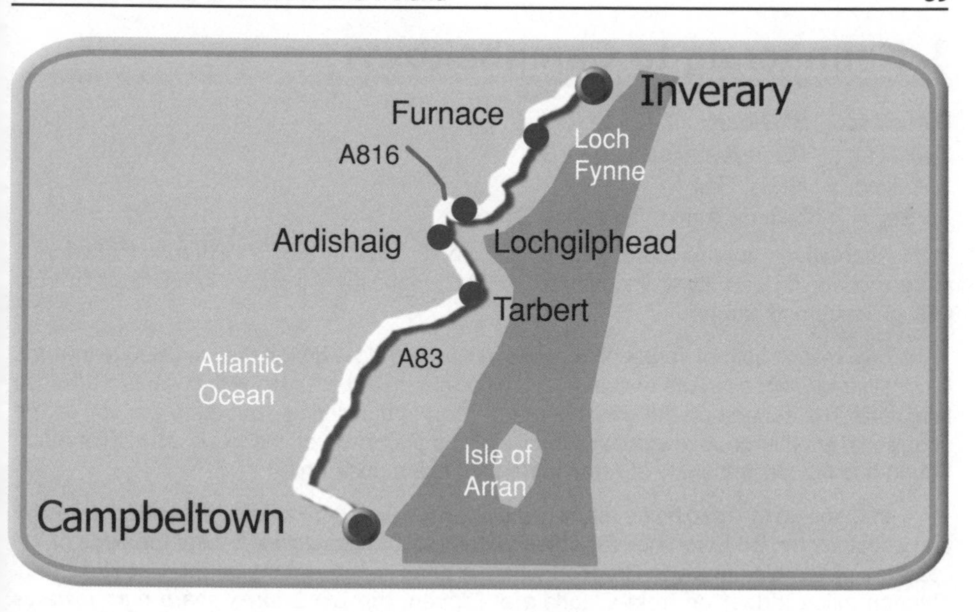

Road	Direction	Comment
A83	Lochgilphead	Head south out of Inverary towards Lochgilphead
A83	Campbeltown	Left at the roundabout (petrol here) and then straight on at the next roundabout in the town centre
A83	Campbeltown	Left at the third roundabout
A83	Cambeltown	Follow the road across the peninsula and down the Atlantic coast to Campbeltown
A83	Campbeltown	Parking on the harbour pier

8. Kennacraig to Campbeltown

Distance: 31 Miles
Surface: Poor/Average
Scenery: Hills, Sea
To See: Isle of Arran, Skipness Castle

Alternatively, try this route to Campbeltown. It's another single track road that offers a more challenging and rewarding way to get to Campbeltown if you're heading south from Lochgilphead and Tarbet.

Five miles south of Tarbet on the A83 at Kennacraig, turn left onto the B8001 towards Claonaig and Skipness. The next eighteen miles is single-track road with passing places, so take care. The surface on the whole is pretty good - considering - but there are one or two dodgy bits, another good reason for exercising caution. However, the views down Kilbrannan Sound and across to the Isle of Arran more than make up for this.

In Claonaig the road bears round to the right (turn left for Skipness Point and the Castle) and becomes the B842 for the rest of the journey to Campbeltown. It hugs the edge of the coastline all the way down to Grogport where it turns inland, cutting off the views of Arran. Thirteen miles further on from Claonaig at Dippen, the B842 turns sharp right towards Campbeltown, with Carradale straight on, and the single-track road comes to an end. But it's still no two-lane superhighway. There's a petrol station-cum-post office-cum-general store here, as well as a tea room where you can take a well earned break. The remaining thirteen miles provide some interesting and challenging riding, including a few very tight and steep 180 degree hairpins, and some of them don't have very good surfaces!

Entering Campbeltown around the north side of the bay, you should turn left and follow signs to the town centre. Park up on the small pier next to the tourist information office.

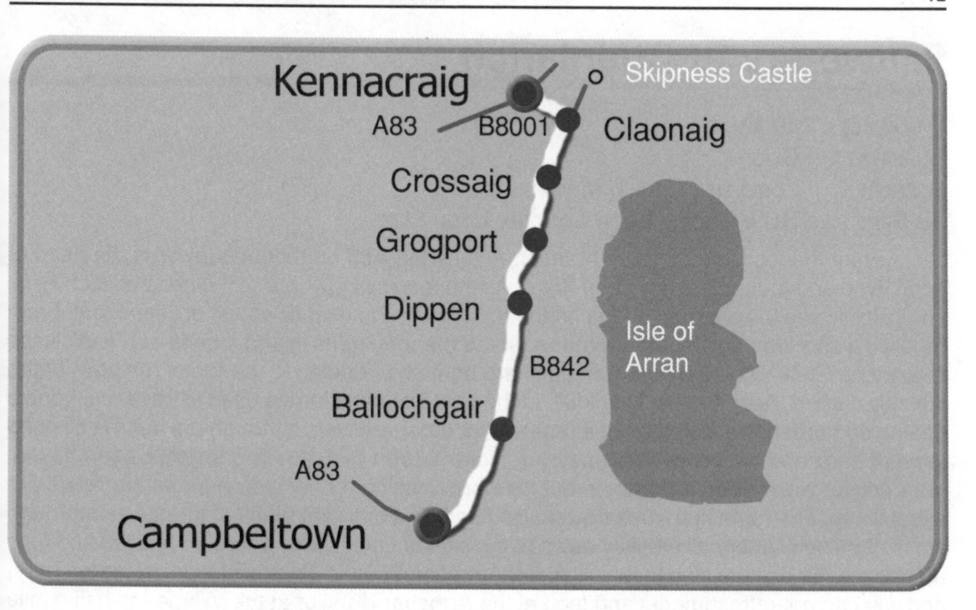

Road	Direction	Comment
B8001	Skipness Claonaig	Turn left 5 miles south of Tarbert onto the B8001 a single track road
B842	Cambeltown	B8001 becomes the B842 at Claonaig. Follow the road all the way down th coast to Cambeltown. Interesting steep and tight hairpin bends so take care

9. Inverary to Crianlarich

Distance: **40 Miles**
Surface: **Good**
Scenery: **Forestry, Lochs, Mountains**
To See: **Glen Croe, Loch Lomond, Loch Fyne**

From the lochside car park at Inverary take the A83 northbound towards the head of Loch Fyne and around the tiny Loch Shira. As the road swings around the head of Loch Fyne you can still see the old road bridge on the right where the river flows out of Glen Fyne. From here it's a short run down past Cairndow where the road turns inland, opens out, and climbs straight up Glen Kinglas before turning sharp right and heading to the top of the pass at the suitably named 'Rest and Be Thankful'. In the past, cars and lorries used to have real trouble getting up here; nowadays it's not a problem for most vehicles, although big trucks still need to work hard and 'rent-a-wrecks' may not make it even though the gradient's been eased. Your engine won't need a breather, but it's worth making a brief stop here as the views are exceptional. The route then runs down Glen Croe on a cracking piece of tarmac and through some startling scenery all the way down to the side of Loch Long, where it turns left and runs around the head of the loch to the village of Arrochar. There's a petrol station on the left here, and you can get refreshments and food at the Arrochar Hotel or at the Village Inn half a mile down the A814 towards Garelochhead, which also has dramatic views down Loch Long to the sea.

Stay on the A83 as it turns left and crosses the narrow isthmus to the west shore of Loch Lomond. In Tarbet turn left at the T-junction and follow the A82 north along the shores of Loch Lomond to Crianlarich. The next few miles are narrow and twisty and the surface is a bit iffy in places. There's also a lot of trees overhanging the road which keeps the tarmac wet long after the rain's stopped, so take it easy until you get past the head of the loch and the road starts to climb into Glen Falloch. Here, the road and the scenery opens out again, so if you've been stuck behind slow-moving traffic, you can now get a move on. But don't go too quick or you'll miss the outstanding views across to Ben Lui (3,708 ft.) on the left and Ben More (3,708 ft.) on the right. Catch them before the road drops down into Crianlarich and meets the A82/85 at a T-junction. There's not a lot here, so you should either turn left for Tyndrum, Glen Coe and Fort William, or right for Lochearnhead and Callander. Of course you could always turn around and go all the way back to Inverary.

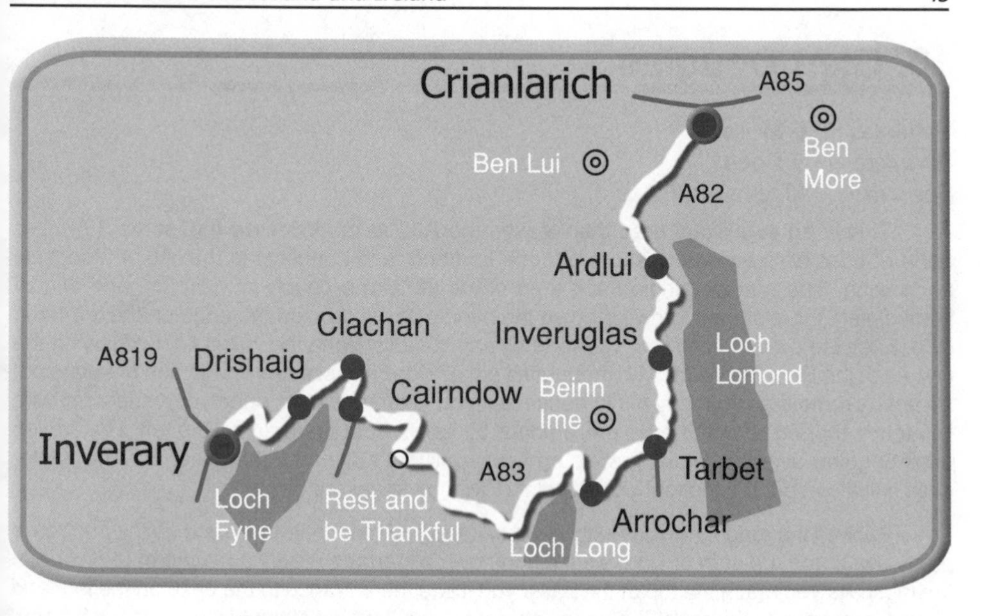

Road	Direction	Comment
A83	Tarbet	Head north out of Inverary around the head of Loch Fyne
A83	Tarbet	Climb up Glen Kinglas to the 'Rest and be Thankful' and on towards Arrochar (petrol station) and Tarbet
A82	Crianlarich	Left at the junction with the A82 along the shore of Loch Lomond
A82	Crianlarich	At Crianlarich turn left on the A82 Tyndrum, Glen Coe and Fort William. Right for Lochearnhead or Callandar

10. Glen Douglas

Distance: 6 Miles
Surface: V Poor
Scenery: Mountains, Fells

This is an ex-military road than leaves the A82 at the Inverbeg Inn, some 3½ miles north of Luss on the western shore of Loch Lomond, and connects to the A814 alongside Loch Long. The narrow, single-track road starts off with a couple of hairpins, and almost immediately there's grass growing down the middle and a drop off the edge on the left-hand side. Exercise extreme caution. The road climbs steadily along the valley floor, following the course of the Douglas Water with mountains either side. The scenery is wild and desolate but it's not as remote as you may think, because if you keep your eyes open you'll see a tall wire link fence topped off with barbed wire about 50 yards from the road on the left. Don't even think of going over the top as there's an active military base the other side, and the eagle-eyed will also spot the lookout posts and the Tannoy speakers on poles.

Back to the road, and you really need to keep your concentration here as the surface is pretty awful and the strip of what we'll laughingly call tarmac is only a couple of feet wide at the most. As you reach the top of the pass, you'll see the entrance to the base on the left, and almost immediately the road(?) plunges straight down the side of the hill towards Loch Long. And then just before you reach the bottom, there's a couple of hairpin bends, with the last one depositing you straight onto the main road, which fortunately is not very busy!

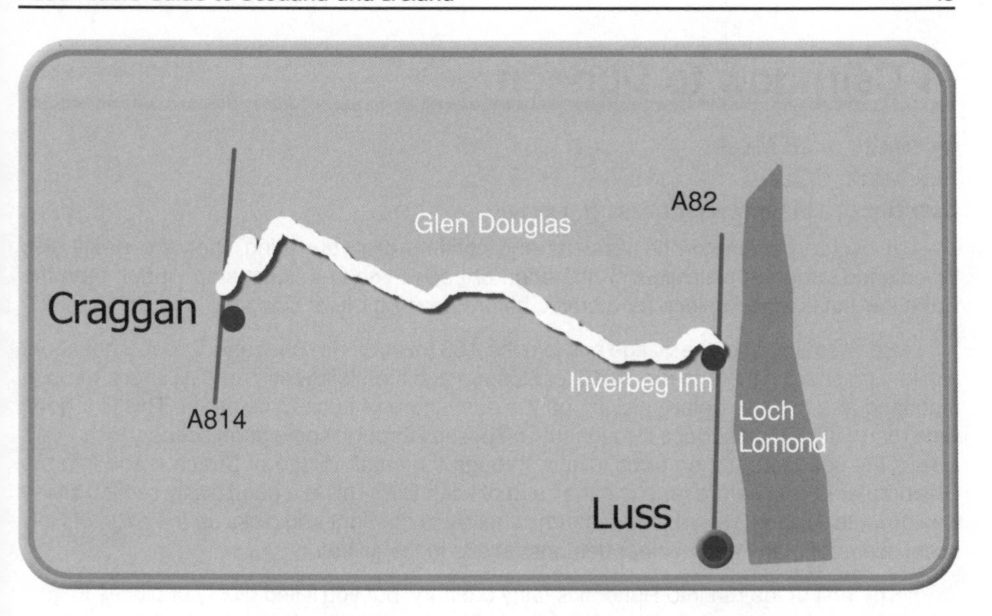

Road	Direction	Comment
A82	Tarbet	From Luss turn left after $3^1/_2$ miles opposite the Inverbeg Inn
Unmarked	Craggan	Follow the narrow single tracked road for some spectaular views. Extreme care necessary as the road has grass down the middle and there are some very tight bends.

11 Cairndow to Dunoon

DISTANCE: 28 MILES
SURFACE: GOOD
SCENERY: MOUNTAINS, FORESTRY, LOCHS

If exotic rhododendrons, azaleas and conifers are your thing, then the Ardkinglas Woodland Garden at Cairndow on the edge of Loch Fyne is a 'must stop'. If not, then the Cairndow Inn is a good place for a break, before heading off for Dunoon.

Head south out of the village and join the A83 towards Arrochar and Tarbet. After about a mile, turn sharp right onto the A815 for Dunoon and then follow this road as it runs through moorland and forestry before picking up the east shore of Loch Fyne again. This is a good wide road with a good surface throughout and passes through some great scenery with views across the sea loch. It then turns inland, through the small village of Strachur and into the Glenbranter Forest before reaching the head of Loch Eck. This is a good twisty section all the way down to Ardbeg, where the road turns sharply to the right and picks up the edge of Holy Loch, scene of many anti-nuclear demonstrations in the sixties.

The rest of the run into Dunoon is fairly ordinary, but you'll find plenty of places to stop in the town and get something to eat and drink. The town itself is dominated by a grassy lump of rock known as Castle Hill, topped off by Castle House that was built in the 1820s by a wealthy Glaswegian.

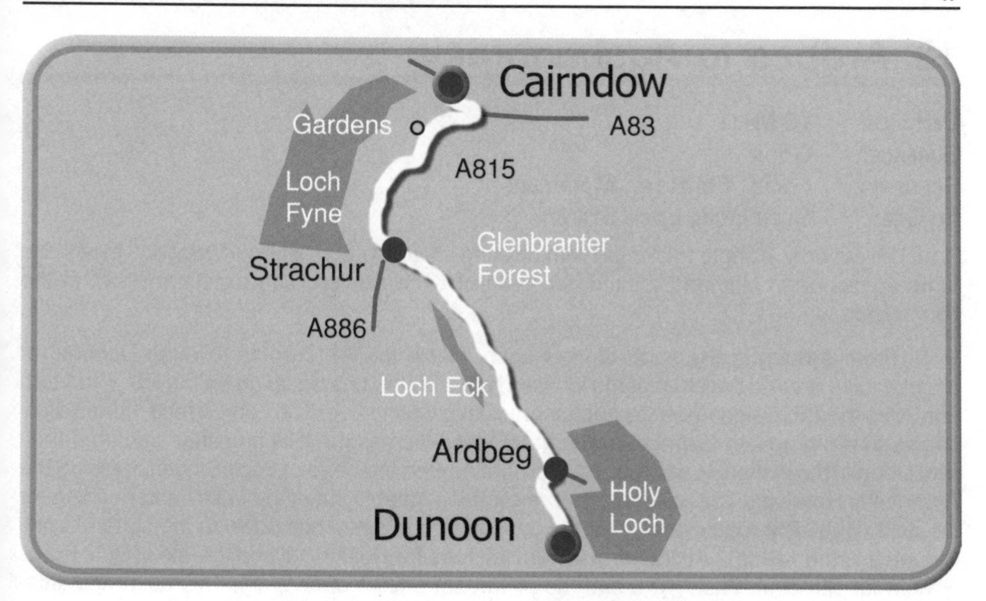

Road	Direction	Comment
A83	Tarbet	Head south out of Cairdow for about 1 mile
A815	Dunoon	Turn sharp right onto the A815 which has great scenery as you follow the shore of Loch Fyne
A815	Dunoon	Good twisty section after Strachur all the way to Ardbeg and then on to Dunoon

12. Ardbeg to Auchenbreck

Distance: 10 Miles
Surface: Good
Scenery: Lochs, Forestry, Mountains
To See: Glen Lean, Loch Striven

This is only a single track road with passing places, but it's well surfaced and twists and turns across open fells and around the head of Loch Striven, with excellent views of the countryside.

From Ardbeg to the north of Holy Loch, follow the A815 south towards Dunoon for about a mile, around the head of the loch and passing the petrol station on the left. Then turn right onto the B836 signposted to Auchenbreck and Colintraive. The narrow road immediately begins to climb up into Glen Lean with great views across the hills on either side, and then drops down into Ardtaraig and turns sharp right around the head of Loch Striven, passing the Ardentinny Hotel and Craigandaive before climbing steeply out of the valley and heading for the next ridge. The road climbs over the pass and then descends down to the head of Loch Ridden and the A815, at Auchenbreck. Turn left here for Colintraive and the isle of Bute Ferry, or right for Strachur, Loch Fyne and the picturesque town of Inverary. This quiet and little-used road traverses some wonderfully remote countryside and if you need any more of an excuse for the journey, why not call in at the Ardentinny Hotel for a snack and a drink if you plan on staying.

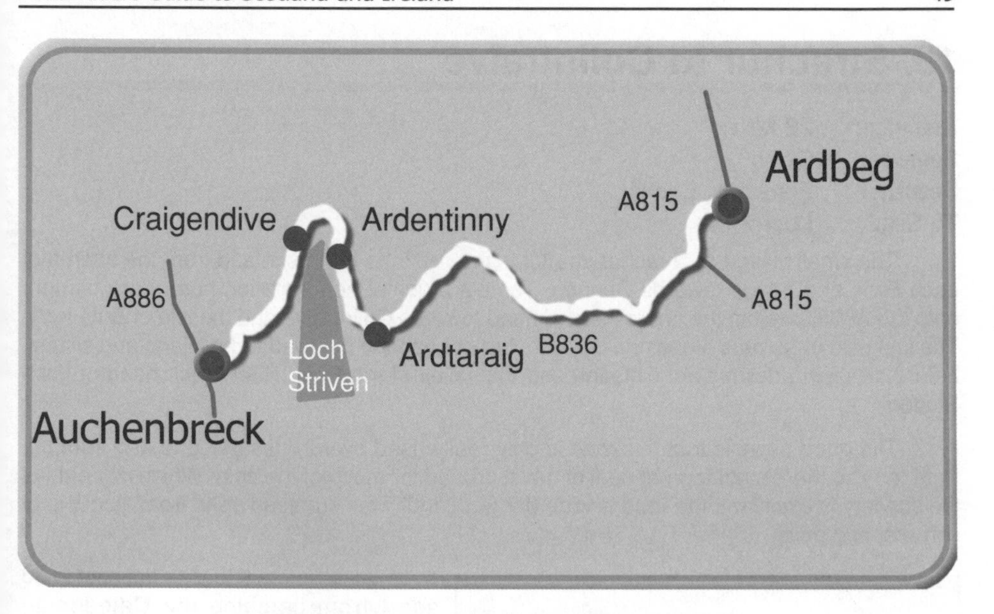

Road	Direction	Comment
A815	Dunoon	Take the A815 from Ardbeg for about 1 mile
B836	Auchenbreck	Turn right onto the B836 and follow this road up over Glen Lean into Ardtaraig
B836	Auchenbreck	At Auchenbreck turn right for Strachur, left for Colintraive and the Isle of Bute Ferrrry

13. Strachur to Colintraive

Distance: 22 Miles
Surface: Good
Scenery: Forestry, Lochs
To See: Loch Fyne

The small village of Strachur straddles the A815 as it turns inland from the shores of Loch Fyne and heads towards Dunoon. There's a useful petrol station here. Turn off right onto the A866 to rejoin the shoreline and head towards Colintraive and the Isle of Bute ferry. The first mile or so runs alongside the loch, but at Leanach the road turns inland and climbs, before sweeping down Caol Ghleann and the valley of the River Ruel to the head of Loch Riddon.

The good news is that this road is only really used by vehicles going to and from the Bute ferry,so there's not a great deal of traffic around for much of the time. Which is great, as the scenery is excellent, the road is wide (for Scotland), well surfaced apart from a couple of corners, and quick.

On the Bute Ferry

At Colintraive there's not a lot to do apart from catching the Caledonian MacBrayne ferry (www.calmac.co.uk) to Bute (www.isle-of-bute.com) across the narrow Kyles of Bute to Rhubodach. The crossing is expensive, but that wouldn't be too bad if there were good roads to ride and some stunning scenery to take in, but there aren't and there isn't. Only the southern 'lowland' part of the island has any road access, and what roads that do exist are narrow and poorly surfaced.

But if that's not enough, the main occupation of the island is agriculture, and unfortunately a lot of it seems to be continuously transferred from the fields to the roads. The capital Rothesay, was once a grand Victorian resort, but it now has a slightly tired and rundown air about it. There is however a good selection of shops and useful services around.

The Highland Boundary Fault runs across the island (and Rothesay) and is marked by the wrought iron arch on the harbourfront. But perhaps Rothesay's greatest claim to fame is its Victorian toilets, built by Twyfords in 1899 and since declared a national treasure!

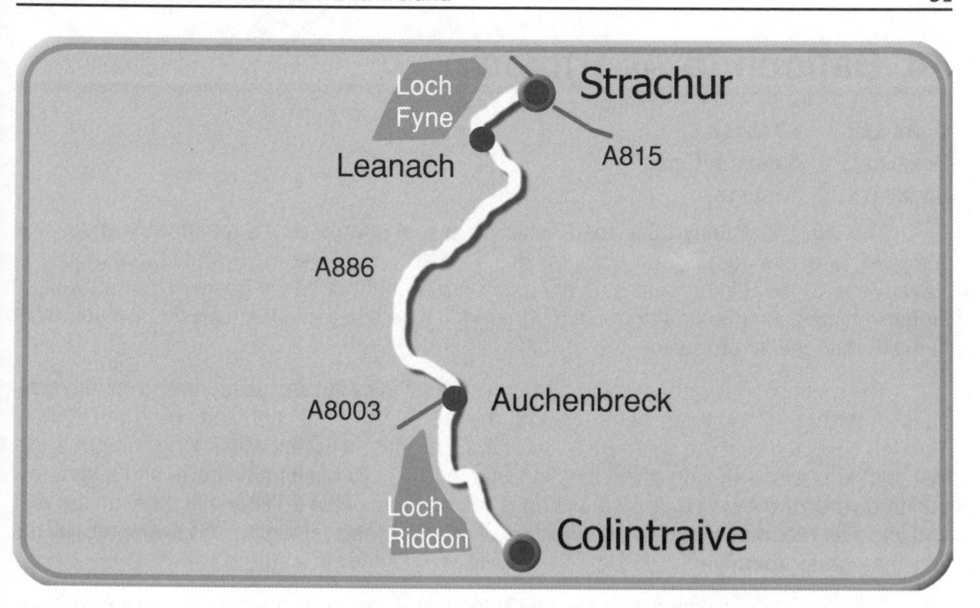

Road	Direction	Comment
A886	Colintraive	Turn off the A815 onto the A886 in Strachur towards Colintrave and the Isle of Bute Ferry
A886	Colintraive	Keep straight on at Leanach and continue through Auchenbreck to Colintraive
		Take the ferry for the Isle of Bute if you wish, where the main interest is the 1899 toilets - now declared a national treasure

14. Balloch to Aberfoyle

Distance: **19 Miles**
Surface: **Average/Good**
Scenery: **Forestry**

The A811 is a fairly busy road, which is a real shame as it's reasonably wide, well surfaced, and has some great corners. But it's also one of the main routes from Faslane Naval Base to the Stirling area so it attracts a fair amount of heavy goods traffic as well as tourist vehicles going to and from Loch Lomond. It's best to avoid the rush hours if you want to make reasonable progress.

The route heads northeast out of Balloch through fairly flat and uninteresting countryside, passing through Gartocharn before joining the A809 at a T-junction just south of Drymen. Turn left here and skirt the southern edge of the Garadhban Forest with a long straight and a fast right-left before arriving at the junction with the A81. Turn left again here, and after a few hundred yards the A811 peels off to the right, taking most of the traffic with it. Stay on the A81 and you'll be met with an excellent selection of bends, crests, straights and sweepers, all the way through to Aberfoyle.

Bear left at the junction with the A873 and follow the road into the centre of Aberfoyle. Take a break here in the large car park on the left behind the Tourist Information Centre, and grab a coffee and scones in the tearoom at the end of the high street.

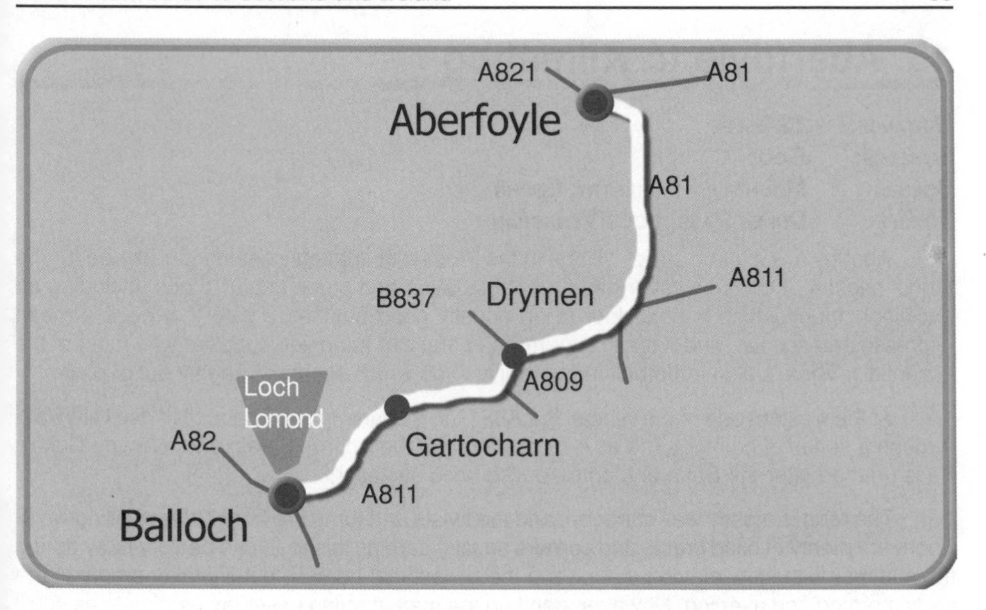

Road	Direction	Comment
A811	Gartocharn Stirling	Follow the A811 through Gartocharn towards Drymen
A809	Drymen	Left onto the A809 just before Drymen
A81	Aberfoyle	Left onto the A81 past Drymen. Stay on the A81 for an excellent ride all the way to Aberfoyle
A837	Aberfoyle	Turn left at the junction of the A81 with the A837 for the centre of Aberfoyle. Car park behind the Tourist Information Centre on the left

15. Aberfoyle to Kilmahog

DISTANCE: **13 MILES**
SURFACE: **GOOD**
SCENERY: **MOUNTAINS, FORESTRY, LOCHS**
TO SEE: **DUKES PASS, LOCH VENACHAR**

Aberfoyle is a 'main street' village in the Trossachs that only seems to wake up for the tourist season. It does however have a petrol station and some useful shops, including an excellent chippy which is next door to an equally good butcher, a café that does a mean espresso and scones, and a small supermarket that can keep you supplied with most of the essentials. There's also a football memorabilia shop which seems strangely out of place.

At the western end of the village, the A821 turns sharp right and launches itself skyward through a series of hairpin turns as it climbs through the Achray Forest and over the Duke's Pass (named after the Duke of Montrose who once owned it).

The road is mostly well surfaced, and the twists and turns are hard but rewarding work. There are plenty of blind crests and corners so take care as this road can be very busy during the summer with slow moving traffic (and the occasional horse!), but it's fairly empty in the early morning and evening. However, don't go too mad at trying to set fastest times, as you'll miss the outstanding views at the top of the pass (there's a viewpoint where you can get excellent views of Ben Venue and Loch Katrine) and the superb woodland scenery.

At the bottom of the pass, a road to Ben Venue (strong walking boots required) and Loch Katrine and its steamer trip leads off to the left, as the route turns sharp right and runs around Loch Achray and through woodland to the hamlet of Brig o' Turk. Then the road runs alongside Loch Venachar, with views across to the Menteith Hills on the right and the 2,882 ft. summit of Ben Ledi (another popular walking destination) on your left. Following the valley, the A821 ends in the small village of Kilmahog and a junction with the A84.

A mile to the right is Callander and all services (fuel at the extreme far end of the town), while turning left will take you through the Pass of Leny and alongside Loch Lubnaig to Lochearnhead. Callander is a very popular summer holiday base and suffers from serious overcrowding as a result. People started flocking to it in their horse-drawn carriages in the 18th & 19th century as a result of the popularity of Sir Walter Scott's and William Wordsworth's writings. Then Queen Victoria chose to visit when the railway arrived and success was assured.

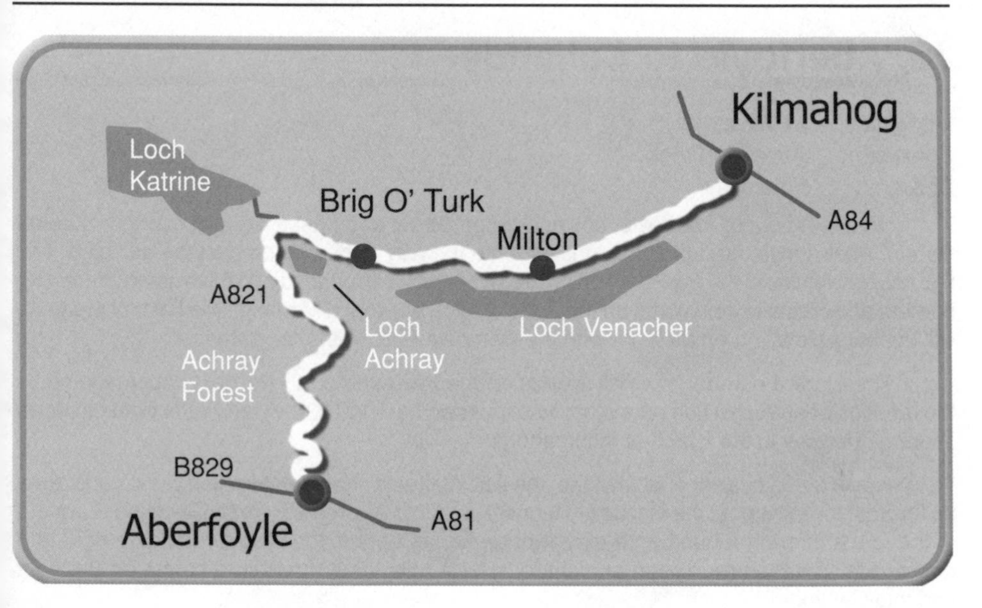

Road	Direction	Comment
A821	Kilmahog	Keep on the A821 out of Aberfoyle and climb up through the hairpins and over Duke's Pass
A821	Kilmahog	Left for the road to Loch Katrine
A821	Kilmahog	Follow the road along Loch Venacher to Kilmahog. Turn right on the A84 for Callander and all main services, left for the Pass of Leny

16. Aberfoyle to Callander

Distance: 11 Miles
Surface: Average/Good
Scenery: Forestry

Head east out of Aberfoyle, down the High Street and past a useful if expensive petrol station. After a mile turn left at the junction onto the A81 and carry on past the golf club. The first couple of miles to the Port of Mentieth are wide and well surfaced and have some interesting corners and crests to help warm up the tyres. As you approach Menteith, the Lake of Menteith will appear below you on the right with the Campsie Fells in the far distance.

There are a number of small islands on the lake, and on the largest, Inchmahome, is the remains of an Augustine priory that was founded back in 1238. A ferry runs from the north shore of the lake to the Island of Inchmahome.

A mile and a quarter past the lake, the A81 makes a sharp left turn and climbs and turns up through forestry, past the Castle of Rednock and into the Torrie Forest. Dropping down out of the forest through a number of excellent sweeping bends, the road turns sharp right at a crossroads and then runs dead straight for over a mile, past the leisure centre on the right and into Callander.

Lake Menteith and the CAmpsie Fells

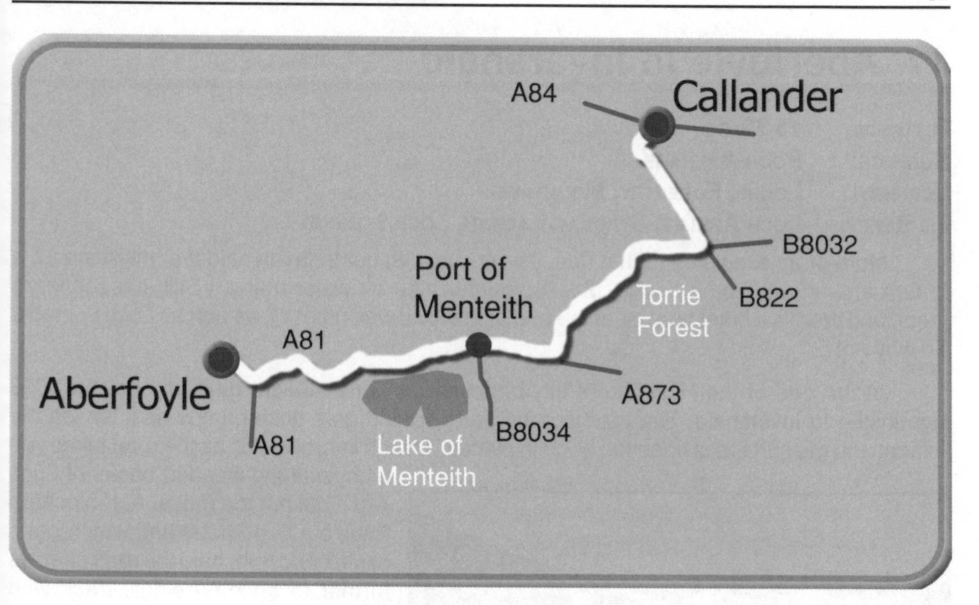

Road	Direction	Comment
A81	Callander	Turn onto the A81 about a mile out of Aberfoyle
A81	Callander	Lake of Mentieth on your right with ferry to the island of Inchmahome
A81	Callander	Sharp left turn about 1$^1/_4$ miles from the end of the lake as the road climbs up through the Torrie Forest
A81	Callander	Left at the crossroads and on into Callander

17. Aberfoyle to Inversnaid

DISTANCE: **15 MILES**
SURFACE: **POOR/AVERAGE**
SCENERY: **LOCHS, FORESTRY, MOUNTAINS**
TO SEE: **LOCH ARKLET, STRONACHLACHAR, LOCH LOMOND**

More of an excursion than a ride, as once you've got to Inversnaid the only way out is to turn around and come back – unless you can ride on water that is!! Still, the scenery's great, and there's a hotel and bar at the end of the road with great views across Loch Lomond. So why not?

At the end of the High Street in Aberfoyle, continue straight on and take the B829 signposted to Inversnaid. The road quickly narrows and gets quite bumpy as it leaves the village, and the surface is none too good in places. Things improve a bit as the road takes you alongside the wooded banks of Loch Ard – but not too much. At Kinlochard there's a large hotel and watersports centre, and from here the road narrows further to become single-track with passing places, and then appears to go through a set of convulsions which at times can bring down the view ahead to as little as fifty feet, so take care. But it's a cracking ride, and when you finally come out of the woods the view down Loch Arklet, with the peaks of Ben Vorlich and Ben Vane in the background, is worth a well-earned breather.

LOCH ARKLETT

Just past here there's a T-junction. Turn right, and there's a short but gravelly run down to Stronachlachar. This is a small hamlet with a jetty at the end of Loch Katrine, whose only real claim to fame is in being the turn round point for the SS Sir Walter Scott that steams along the loch from the foot of Ben Venue on a daily basis during the summer months. Turn left at the T-junction and continue through open country alongside Loch Arklet all the way to the Inversnaid Hotel on the banks of Loch Lomond. Loch Arklet originally emptied into Loch Lomond down a spectacular waterfall, but after being dammed at its western end and the level raised in Victorian times, it now empties into Loch Katrine and assists with the Glasgow water supply.

Be careful for the last mile or so past the dam wall, as the road drops steeply down to the loch through a couple of hairpin turns – and coaches use this road !! There's plenty of parking space in front of the hotel, and you can get refreshments and snacks in the bar or a three-course meal in the restaurant. But just remember you've got to ride back to Aberfoyle. There's a pleasant one mile stroll north alongside Loch Lomond to the old boathouse. Go past the hotel in the other direction to see the remains of the Loch Arklet waterfall.

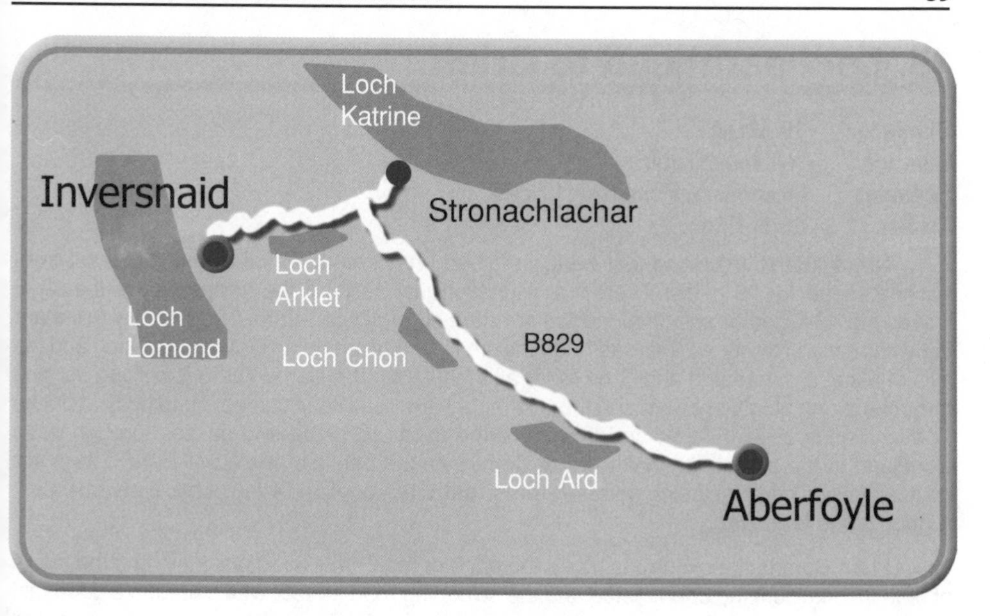

Road	Direction	Comment
B829	Inversnaid	Take the B829 from the end of the High Street in Aberfoyle. Stunning view down Loch Arklet as you emerge from the forest past Loch Chon
B829	Inversnaid	Left at the crossroads for Inversnaid and right for the gravelly road to Stronachlachar
B829	Inversnaid	Continue down the road to Inversnaid and the hotel on the banks of Loch Lomond

18. Lochearnhead to Crieff

Distance: 19 Miles
Surface: Average/Good
Scenery: Mountains, Forestry, Lochs
To See: Loch Earn

No excuses for getting lost here, as all you have to do is follow the A85 east from Lochearnhead for 19 miles. There's a T-junction just north of the village where the A85 leaves the A84, and heads off along the northern edge of Loch Earn. The first few miles are fairly narrow and twisty, as the road hugs the small strip of shoreline between the loch and the hills of Meall a´ Mhadaidh and Sròn Mhór all the way to St. Fillans. There is a good surface throughout and plenty of twists and turns, although the road itself can get quite busy at times. The loch ends at St. Fillans, and from here the road opens out and passes through open woodland to the attractive small town of Comrie on the banks of the River Earn. There are useful services here, including general stores, fuel, a tearoom and even public conveniences. A good place for a stop.

From Comrie, the A85 runs along the edge of the Earn's flood plain giving good views of both the surrounding countryside and the sweeping road ahead, which means a good fast run, traffic permitting, all the way to the bustling town of Crieff. But keep an eye open for the numerous narrow sections where streams run under the road, especially if there's traffic coming the other way. You'll find all the services you could possibly need in Crieff, including a bike tyre depot, but it's not too easy to find somewhere to park.

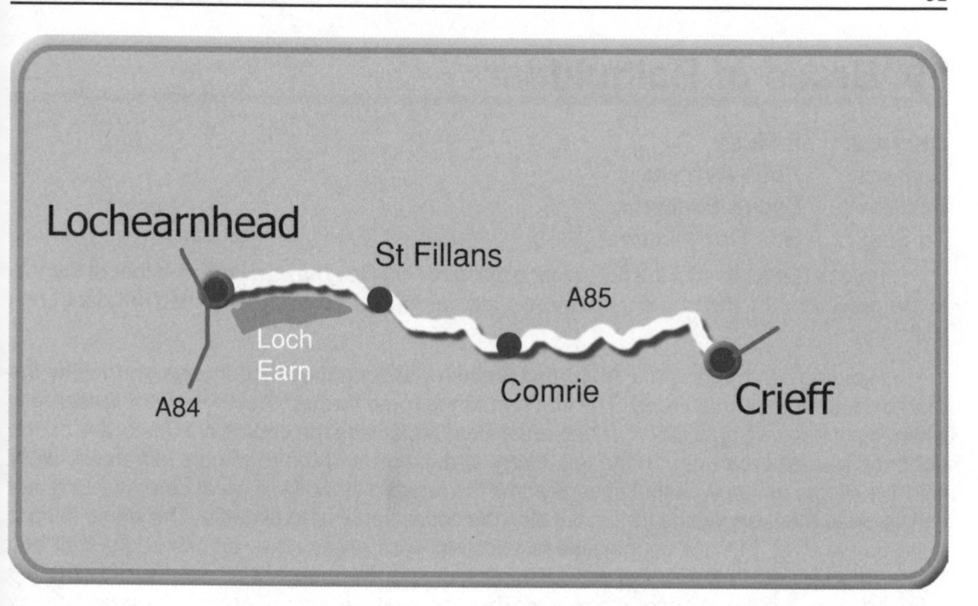

Road	Direction	Comment
A85	Crieff	Take the A85 out of Lochearnhead along the banks of Loch Earn
A85	Crieff	And carry straight on around the twists and turns until you come to Crieff!

19. Braes of Balquidder

Distance: 8 Miles
Surface: Poor/Average
Scenery: Lochs, Forestry,
To See: Rob Roy's Grave

Balquidder's fame as the final resting place of Rob Roy draws a large number of tourists to the graveyard by the church, but there's also a good scenic run to be had out past Loch Voil.

Heading north along the A84 from Stathyre, turn right at Kingshouse and follow the road back under the main road. The first part of the route through Auchtubh is of reasonable width, but it narrows right down as you enter Balquidder with the church and the grave on the right and a useful tearoom on the left. Carry straight on and the road gets extremely twisty with lots of ups and downs that severely limit the forward view. Take great care as you're not only likely to meet oncoming traffic, but also the occassional herd of cattle. The whole thing is quite demanding, but the countryside is excellent with great views across Lochs Voil and Doine to your left. Between the two lochs at Monachiyle, there's a useful hotel that offers refreshments and the chance of a rest, or you can continue on, along an ever deteriorating surface to Inverlochlarig, where you'll find a picnic area, some benches, a shelter, and not much else. Now all you can do is turn around and make your way back to the A84.

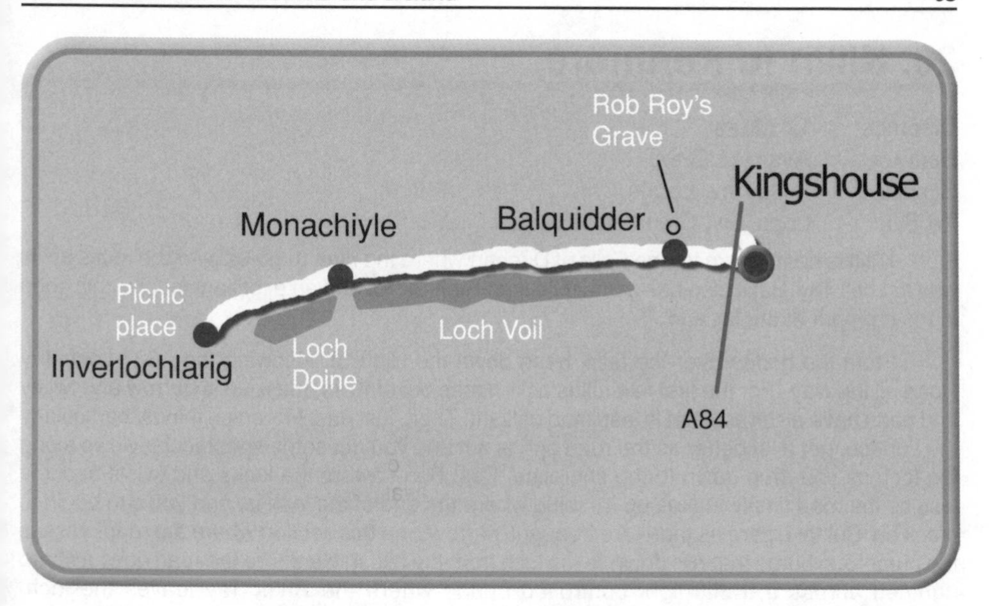

Road	Direction	Comment
Unmarked	Balquidder	Heading north on the A84 turn right at Kingshouse and then back under the A84 for Balquidder
Unmarked	Balquidder	At Balquidder Rob Roy's Grave is on the right
Unmarked	Inverlochlarig	Follow the road past Loch Voile and Loch Doine to Inverlochlarig where there is just a place to have a picnic

20. Killin to Kenmore

DISTANCE: 17 MILES
SURFACE: AVERAGE/GOOD
SCENERY: FORESTRY, LOCHS
TO SEE: LOCH TAY, CRANNOG VILLAGE

Killin is best known for the Falls of Dochart where the river tumbles over the rocks on its way to Loch Tay. But it also has a one mile long High Street and an excellent mobile chip shop in the car park at the far end.

From the bridge over the falls, head down the High St. following the A827 Loch Tay Road all the way. For the first few miles as it climbs out of Killin, the road is narrow and twisty and parts have a surface that is less than brilliant. Then, just past Morenish things, particularly the surface, get a lot better as the road opens out and you get some spectacular views along the loch as you drop down to the shoreline. Past Ben Lawers the kinks and twists become less as the road finally makes up it's mind where the end of the loch is, and you can begin to crack on. But take care as there are frequent 'narrows' on this section where the road crosses the numerous burns that run down to the loch from the hill. At Kenmore the road does a sharp right/left across a traffic light controlled bridge where the River Tay leaves the loch. Refreshments are available just over the other side of the bridge at the Kenmore Hotel, or at a small tearoom-cum-gift shop by the car park. The Crannog Village is up the South Loch Tay Road by the watersports centre.

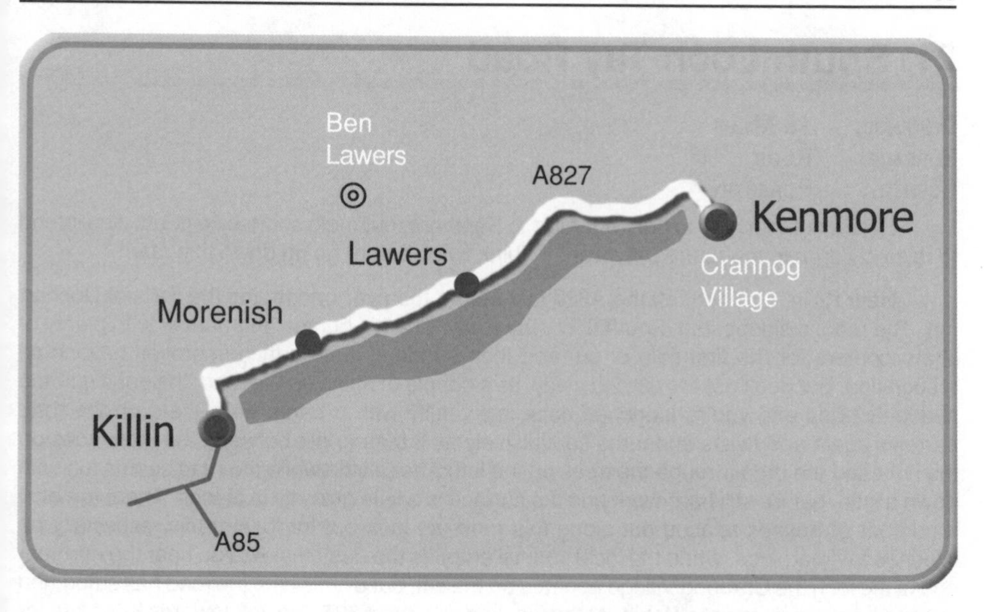

Road	Direction	Comment
A827	Kenmore	From the bridge over the Falls of Dochart, follow Loch Tay Road all the way
A827	Kenmore	Follow the road along the side of Loch Tay for some spectacular views and good riding, all the way to Kenmore
Unmarked	Crannog Village	Follow the South Loch Tay Road from Kenmore to visit the Crannog Village and the watersports centre

21. South Loch Tay Road

Distance: **18 Miles**
Surface: **Poor**
Scenery: Forestry

Here's another way to get from Killin to Kenmore, but male sportsbike riders who intend to raise children in the future may want to think twice before going down this road!

Near Killin, turn right off the A827 just before the river bridge and the Falls of Dochart Inn. The road is signposted 'South Loch Tay Road' and it's bumpy and narrow with plenty of sharp corners for the first mile or so, and then suddenly the surface improves beyond all recognition. But don't get too carried away, as a couple of miles up the road, the good surface suddenly ends and you're launched back into reality with a bang. From here on the road narrows again and twists and turns convulsively as it tries to get between the rock faces on the right and the drop through the trees on the left! After a little while the road seems to settle down a little, but it's still hard work and the surface is a little gravelly in places. There are also a number of houses spaced out along this road, so look out for local traffic, especially on Wednesday mornings, when the local council empties the dustbins! As you near the northern end of the loch the Crannog Village appears on the left, but by this time the road has smoothed out and become quite acceptable. At the junction with the A827, turn left towards Kenmore for a well-earned break.

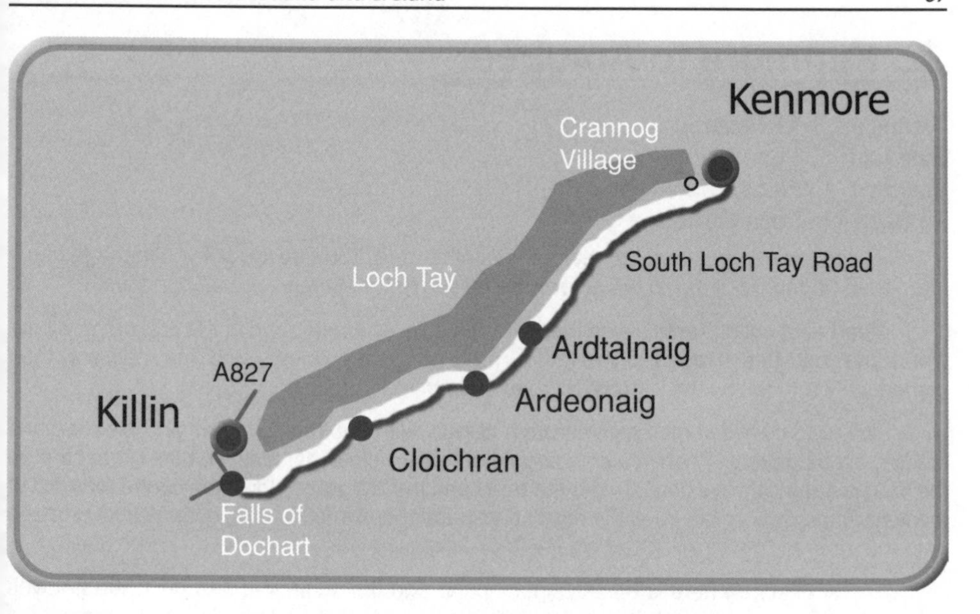

Road	Direction	Comment
A827	South	Just out of Killin heading south turn off the A827 just before the bridge. The road is signed South Loch Tay Road
Unmarked	Kenmore	Follow the road around the south side of Loch Tay all the way to Kenmore. As you approach Kenmore the Crannog Village is on the left
A827	Kenmore	Turn left at the junction with the A827 to go to the centre of Kenmore

22. Kenmore to Amulree

Distance: 11 Miles
Surface: Poor
Scenery: Fells, Mountains
To See: Loch Quaich

A single track road, and it's not for the fainthearted. You'll be lucky if you manage much more than 30 mph, but the views across the fells to the mountains are stupendous.

Head east out of Kenmore on the A827 towards Aberfeldy, and at the end of the village where the road bears round to the left, turn right onto the South Loch Tay road and then immediately turn left up the narrow(er) road signposted 'Amulree'.

The road climbs immediately through woods, with the trees overhanging the road and making it a bit gloomy. There's also a couple of really vicious hairpins, so take great care as the road is nearly always damp under the trees and there's gravel down the centre for most of the way. Once clear of the trees the road heads straight up into the hills, over a cattle grid and onto the moors.

The scenery up here is bleakly spectacular and the summit at around 1,800 ft. gives some superb views, although I wouldn't like to be up here in the winter. From the summit the road descends rapidly, crossing the River Quaich over a small stone bridge at the hamlet of Garrow, and then running through open country along Glen Quaich and Loch Freuchie until it finishes at a junction with the A822 at Amulree.

On the Moors above Kenmore

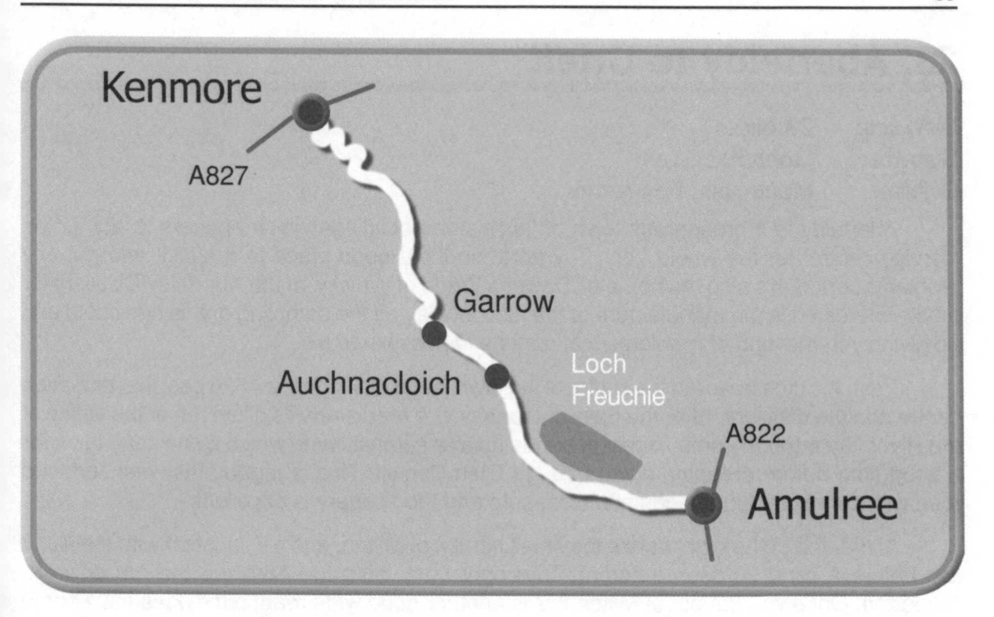

Road	Direction	Comment
A827	Aberfeldy	Head east out of Kenmore and at the end of the village turn right onto the South Loch Tay Road
Unmarked	Amulree	Immediately turn left up the narrow road marked Amulree. Take care the road has gravel down the centre and there are some sharp hairpin bends, but the scenery is wonderful if on the bleak side
Unmarked	Amulree	Follow the road through Garrow and Auchnacloich to Amulree and the junction with the A822

23. Aberfeldy to Crieff

Distance: 23 Miles
Surface: Good/Excellent
Scenery: Mountains, Forrestry

Aberfeldy is a prosperous town of large stone buildings which appears to act as the 'service centre' for the whole Loch Tay area, so it's a good place to re-stock and get any problems sorted. It's also the home of 'Dewar's World of Whisky' at the Aberfeldy Distillery for those interested in the manufacture of the malt; but lay off the sampling or this ride could end up giving you the kind of problems that may be impossible to fix!

From the crossroads in the centre of the town, head south on the A826 past the recreation centre and the distillery. After the Falls of Moness, the road starts its climb out of the valley of the River Tay through some excellent bends up to a summit level, which it only maintains for a short time before dropping down through Glen Cochill. This is a good fast well surfaced road with some cracking bends and sweepers and the scenery is excellent.

At the end of the glen there's the small hamlet of Milton, and a T-junction with the A822 just before a blind 90-degree corner. Turn right here, onto the A822 for the run down to Gilmerton. Once you get out of Milton this is another good wide road, but it does have some dodgy surfaces on a few of the corners, of which there are an awful lot. Some sweep, some bend, and some... "Jeez - where did that go?" So exercise a bit of caution. Concentration levels are not helped by the fact that the scenery is really excellent all along this stretch, with the section from Newton along Sma Glen being particularly memorable.

At Gilmerton there's another T-junction just before a blind 90-degree corner (it must be written into the local road building handbook) and once again you should turn right, this time onto the A85 for the short run into Crieff.

This large town has all main services, with a busy shopping centre that can cause parking difficulties; but there's a useful petrol station on the right on the way in. Crieff is an old spa town that used to be a cattle trading centre in the 18th century. It really expanded in 1856 when the railway arrived and most of the buildings date from this time, there being some particularly fine Victorian and Edwardian examples.

However, the cattle traders had different priorities and their bargaining was probably assisted no end by the setting up of the Glenturret Distillery to the west of Crieff in 1775. This is the oldest distillery in Scotland and is well worth a visit if only for its splendid isolation, although it's now part of one of the major corporates and home of the 'Famous Grouse' brand.

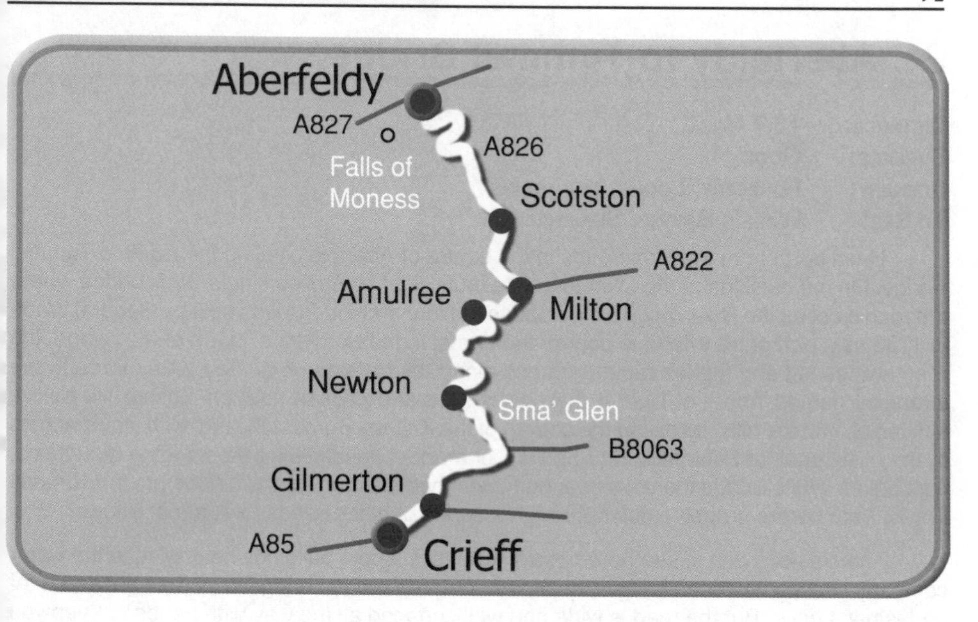

Road	Direction	Comment
A826	Milton	From the crossroads in the town centre take the A826 south past the distillery. Good sweeping bends on a well surfaced road
A826	Milton	Turn right at the T-junction at Milton onto the A822
A822	Crieff	The road twists and turns as it goes along through some beautiful scenery to the T-junction with the A85 at Gilmerton
A85	Crieff	Turn right onto the A85 and continue on to Crieff and the oldest distillery in Scotland

24. Aberfeldy to Tummel Bridge

Distance: 13.7 Miles
Surface: Good
Scenery: Forestry, Lochs, Mountains
To See: Wade's Bridge, Schiehallion

Head north from the crossroads in the centre of Aberfeldy, taking the A846 to Tummel Bridge. On the outskirts of the town there's a traffic light controlled single-track bridge where the road crosses the River Tay. This humpbacked four arch bridge was built by General Wade in 1733 as a part of his efforts to control the unrest in the Highlands. North of the bridge, the road swings left and makes rapid progress along the far side of the Tay valley through the strangely named Appin of Dull. It then turns right and passes through Coshieville before striking up into the hills, following the course of the Keltney Burn on the left, with views across to the misty peak of Schiehallion (3,520 ft.), one of Scotland's few free-standing mountains. Just before White Bridge there's a deer park, and then the road climbs further into the Tummel Forest Park before dropping down through a series of quick bends to Tummel Bridge.

There's not much to see here but a few houses, some buildings belonging to the water company and the new road bridge (the old narrow high-arched bridge is on the right and is for pedestrians only). But the road is wide and well surfaced all the way with bends to keep you occupied and some excellent views across the hills.

Tummel Bridge

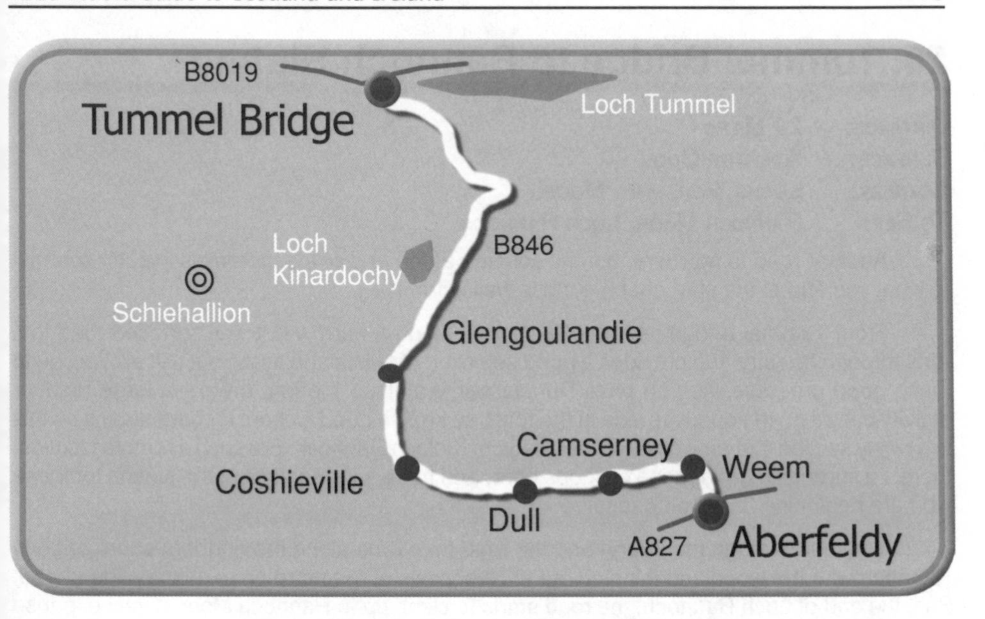

Road	Direction	Comment
B846	Tummel Bridge	Head north from the crossroads in the town centre taking the B846 to Tummel Bridge
B846	Tummel Bridge	Keep on the road along the Appin of Dull and past Coshieville up into the hills before descending into Tummel Bridge

25. Tummel Bridge to Rannoch Station

Distance: 24 Miles
Surface: Average/Good
Scenery: Lochs, Forestry, Moors
To See: Rannoch Moor, Loch Rannoch

Another road to nowhere, but the scenery at the end of the journey is in such contrast to what you find at the start, that the trip is well worth it.

From Tummel Bridge take the B846 west along a narrow but well surfaced road that runs through forestry and provides a good selection of twists and turns, but still allows you to make good progress. As you pass Dunalastair Water on the left, there's a large outdoor activity centre on the opposite side of the road, so keep a good lookout for pedestrians as this is a twisty section that runs down to the village of Kinloch Rannoch. For such a remote location, there's a surprising good range of shops here, and more importantly a petrol station for those who are beginning to run onto reserve.

Continue through the village and the road then runs along the northern shore of Loch Rannoch with the woodland thinning out to give views of the more open countryside ahead. Past the end of Loch Rannoch, the road starts to climb up to Rannoch Moor, a vast expanse of bog and heather, and everything begins to get a bit bleak and windswept, even on a summer's day. By Loch Eigheach there's a small bridge where you can get a good view of the dam and power station, which must be a very daunting place to work in the winter. A little further on, a second bridge takes you over a small burn and up to the settlement at Rannoch Station. This is a stop on the West Highland Line, one of the most scenic railway journeys in the UK. Trains run from Glasgow, through Rannoch, and onto Fort William and Mallaig.

There's a tearoom on the station platform, or you could try the aptly named Midge Bar in the nearby hotel before you retrace your wheeltracks back to civilisation.

Rannoch Station - Time for a Rest

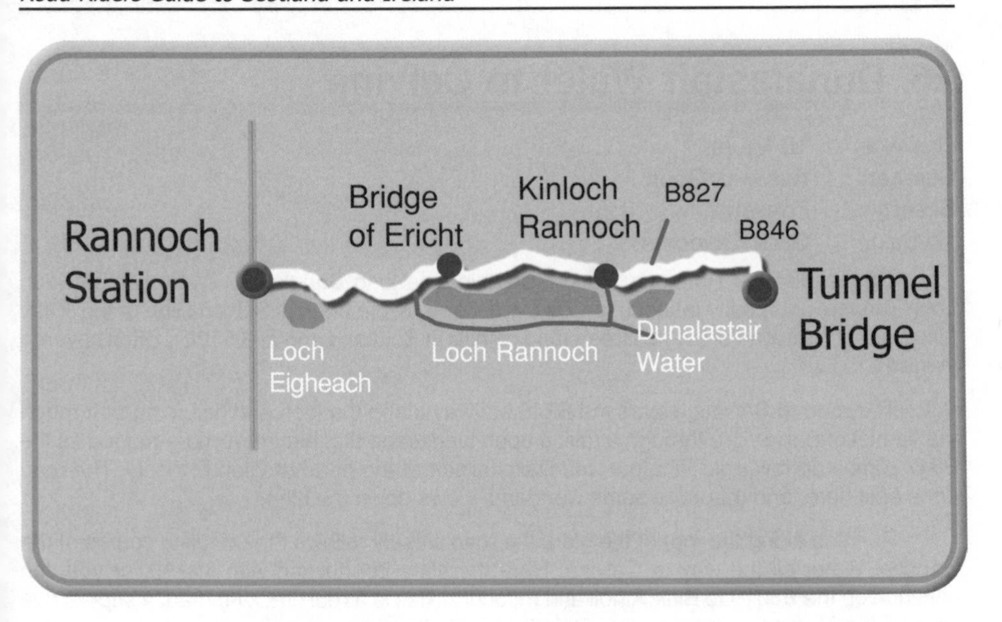

Road	Direction	Comment
B846	Kinloch Rannoch	Follow the B846 out of Tummel Bridge to Kinloch Rannoch where there is a petrol station
B846	Rannoch Station	The road runs along the north of Loch Rannoch and then up onto Rannoch Moor past the dam at Loch Eigheach and on to Rannoch Station and, quite literally, the end of the road. *(When you return you can go down the south of Loch Rannoch on a rather narrow, unmarked road)*

26. Dunalastair Water to Calvine

Distance: **10 Miles**
Surface: **Average/Good**
Scenery: **Forestry**
To See: **Glen Errochty**

On the B846 to Rannoch Station, the two mile long Dunalastair Water lies between Loch Tummel and Loch Rannoch, and is overlooked by the peak of Schiehallion or the 'Fairy Mountain'. This is one of the few free-standing hills in Scotland and at 3,520ft is often covered in mist.

The road to Calvine leaves the B846 halfway along the loch and heads north through the hamlet of Balliemore through a rolling open landscape that becomes more rugged as the B847 climbs up towards Trinafour and Dallchalloch at the head of Glen Errochty. The road turns east here, and there are some wonderful views down the glen.

Running along the foot of the glen, the road closely follows the rambling course of the Errochty Water all the way to Calvine. Here there's a connection with the A9, or you can continue on the B8079 to Blair Atholl and Pitlochry. This is a real cracking road, a superb ride up from the Tummel valley and into Glen Errochty. It's wide and well surfaced with very little traffic, and it twists and turns through some excellent mountain scenery. Definitely one to enjoy.

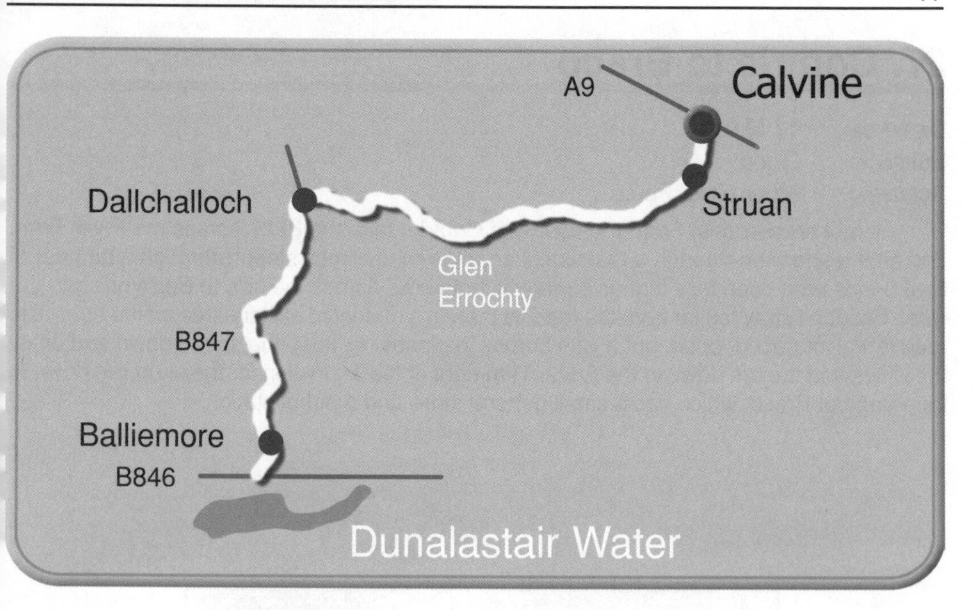

Road	Direction	Comment
B846	Rannoch Station	Leave the B846 halfway along Dunalastair Water by turning onto the B847 to Calvine
B847	Calvine	Follow the B847 through Dallchaloch and into Glen Errochty for some stunning views
B847	Calvine	The road runs along the foot of the glen with some really excellent riding. At Calvine the road meets the A9

27. Comrie to Braco

Distance: **11 Miles**
Surface: **Good**
Scenery: **Mountains, Fells**

A real cracker this. From the centre of Comrie, take the B827 across the River Earn, and after a short run through a residential area the road climbs steeply through a number of tight bends onto open fells that give magnificent views across the hills to Ben Vorlich to the west. But don't stray too far from the road as there's a restricted military area on the right. The road is well surfaced, open, but a little bumpy in places, so keep the speed down and enjoy the views and the run down to the A822. Turn right at the T-junction for the short run down to the village of Braco, which has a small general store and a petrol station.

High on the fells above Comrie

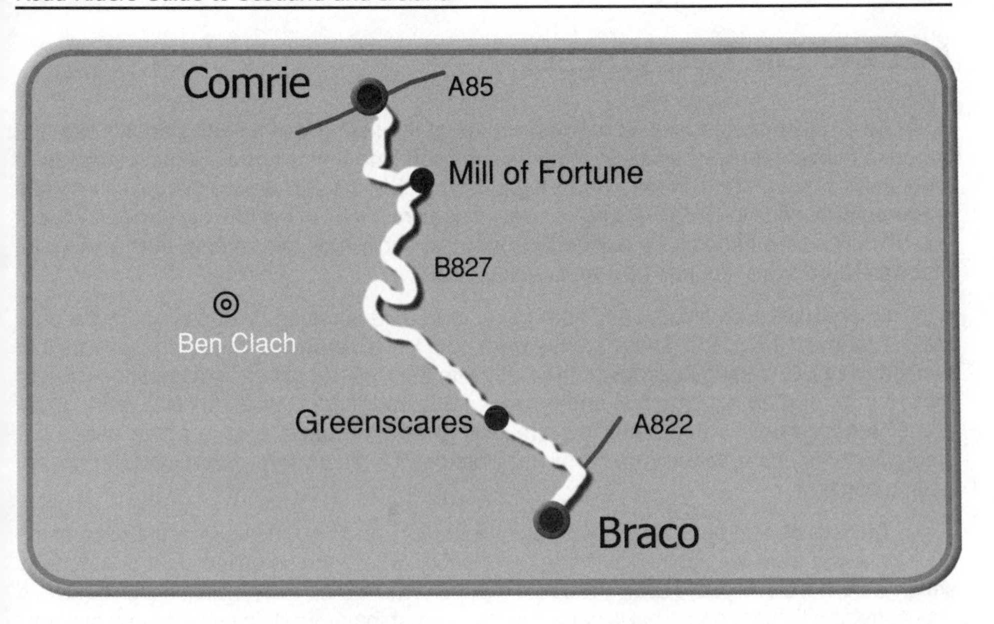

Road	Direction	Comment
B827	Comrie	From the centre of Comrie take the B827 across the River Earn to Comrie
B827	Comrie	A wonderful run all the way down to the junction with the A822 where you turn right
A822	Comrie	Turn right at the junction and follow the road to Comrie

Ireland On Two Wheels

Ah . . the Emerald Isle, so called because of the lush green countryside. It's like that because there's plenty of water to make things grow and it won't come as any surprise to know that it all comes from the sky. In fact there's so much of the stuff around that the countryside is littered with lochs to store the surplus. Yes, it does rain a lot in Ireland, but don't let this put you off making the trip as it's a wonderful country to explore on two wheels. Just make sure that waterproofs are number 1 on your packing list!

Bikers have also shied away from going to Ireland because of stories about the poor state of many of the roads. These stories were true! However, in recent years it appears that bucketfuls of EC funding have found their way into the Department of Transport coffers, and there's a lot of road construction and improvement work under way. This isn't going to be completed overnight (remember, we are talking Ireland here), and in some cases the 'improvements' have actually made things worse in the short term. But overall things are getting better.

The real appeal of Ireland, apart from the scenery and the Guinness, is the pace of the country. Away from the centres of Belfast and Dublin where the so-called 'tiger economy' is self-evident in the everyday hustle and bustle of city life, there's still a very relaxed and measured way to getting things done. This is not a country for rushing around. In fact it's been said that the Spanish concept of mañana conveyed too much of a sense of urgency for the Irish!

Geography

Ireland has often been described as being basin or saucer-shaped, but that's not completely accurate. While the central area is low-lying, it's not a true plain and the uplands don't form a continuous ring around it. In fact the main highland areas show obvious connections to similar features found in the rest of Great Britain, as the three great series of earth movements that shaped the relief of Europe all affected Ireland and ultimately caused its separation from the British mainland. The minor surface features over most of the country were produced during the Ice Age, when the glaciers swept down from the Arctic Circle. The biggest geological difference between Ireland and its larger neighbour is the almost complete absence of the New Red Sandstone, chalk and clay layers that would be laid down in the post-Carboniferous era.

In the northwest of the country around Donegal and Connaught there are areas of low, peat-covered moorland granite plateaus, through which rise isolated quartzite peaks or ridges separated by deep valleys. At the coast where the quartzite beds are exposed, they form the most amazing cliffs which reach heights of almost 2,000 ft. on Achil Island and Slieve League. Although the same rocks also exist on the eastern side of the country, their character is completely different. With the exception of the granitic Mourne mountains, this is a region of low rolling hills interspersed by deep glaciated valleys.

To the southwest the landscape is largely formed by simple folds of Old Red Sandstone with softer Carboniferous rocks in the valley floors between the parallel ridges. This area extends from the Barrow right the way through to the Kerry coast, and is responsible for the spectacular scenery that is found in this part of the country. On a smaller scale, these ridges also run across the southern part of the central lowland. This 'Irish Basin' has an almost undisturbed rock floor that was laid down in the Carboniferous era and since that time has become covered with drift of varying thicknesses. In the north this drift was shaped by the descending ice sheets to form low, rounded humps called drumlins, that extend from Belfast Lough and Dundalk, right across to Sligo. South of the drumlin belt are found long winding gravelly ridges called eskers, that were formed by the melt water from the receding ice sheets at the end of the Ice Age. These streams also brought down boulder clay and limestone fragments that weathered to form the fertile soil of the central plain area. In the far north east, the basalt plateau has steep edges that cut into the coastal glens of Antrim and the columnar cliffs of the Giant's Causeway.

Irish rivers are generally sluggish streams that wander through the marshes and lakes of the drift covered low-lying central region, but as they approach the sea they become more vigorous as their rate of fall increases dramatically. The hydroelectric stations at Ardnacrusha on the Shannon and Ballyshannon on the Erne take advantage of this geography to generate significant amounts of electrical power. In the south of Ireland, the rivers are more closely related to the structure of the country, whilst in the west there are numerous underground streams through limestone areas, the hidden connection between Lough Mask and Lough Corrib being a notable example.

The climate in Ireland is largely determined by its insular position and the prevailing southwesterly airstream. This gives the country a small temperature range of only around 11°C, mean winter and summer temperatures of 6°C and 16°C respectively, but also results in a frequent and abundant rainfall. This can be between 30 and 50 inches each year depending on the part of the country, and you can expect showers of some sort on around two-thirds of the days in a year. Don't say I didn't tell you to take your waterproofs with you.

Getting There

Ireland is an island (surprising that!), and there's no road bridge or tunnels to the rest of the UK. So unless you've got a way of packing your bike into the hold of an aeroplane, you'll be travelling there by ferry. There's plenty of choice for the traveller with services from ports in England, Wales and Scotland to destinations in Northern Ireland and Eire, and even a summer service between Cobh (nr. Cork) and ports in northern France.

From Scotland there are regular sailings from Stranraer to Larne and Belfast in Northern Ireland, with Belfast also being the destination of vessels from Liverpool. If you're a TT fanatic, then ferries sail from Douglas on the Isle of Man to Dublin and Belfast in the summer so you could take a trip after watching the races.

The most popular crossings to Ireland are the services between Holyhead on the Isle of Anglesey off the north Wales coast, and Dublin and Dun Loghaire (six miles south of Dublin) in Eire. If south Wales is closer to home, then there are ferry services between Fishguard or Pembroke and Rosslare in County Wexford. The ferries to Ireland are listed in the table on the next page.

What to See

After many years of being a country that was a little bit quaint, somewhat off the beaten track, and not quite in the same century as other parts of the UK, Ireland discovered that its 'Irishness', and particularly its pub-culture, was a marketable commodity in the rest of the world. A spin-off from this enterprise has been a significant increase in tourism, with the result that some parts of the country can be at a standstill with tourist traffic during the holiday season.

Ferry Operator	Route	Details	Phone	Website
Stena Line	Holyhead - Dublin Fishguard - Rosslaire Fishguard - Rosslaire Holyhead - Dun Laoghaire Stranraer - Belfast Stranraer - Belfast	Ferry 180 mins Ferry 210 mins Ferry 110 mins HSS 99 mins Ferry 195 mins HSS 105 mins	08705 707070	www.stena-line.com
Irish Ferries	Pembroke - Rosslare	Ferry 225 mins	08705 171717	www.irishferries.com
Swansea Cork Ferries	Swansea - Cork	Night Ferry 10hrs	01792 456116	www.swansea-cork.ie
P&O Irish Ferries	Cherbourg - Rosslaire Cherbourg - Dublin Liverpool - Dublin Larne - Cairnryan Larne - Cairnryan Mostyn - Dublin	Night Ferry 18hrs Night Ferry 18hrs Ferry 7-8 hrs Ferry 105 mins HSS 60 mins Ferry 6 hrs	0870 2424777	wwwpoirishsea.com
Brittany Ferries	Cork - Rostoff	Night Ferry 14hrs	021 427 7801	www.brittanyferries.ie
The Steam Pcket Co	Belfast - Troon Belfast - Heysham Douglas - Belfast Douglas - Dublin Liverpool - Dublin	Seacat Summer only Apr-Oct 165 mins Apr-Oct 165 mins ?	01624 645620	www.steam-packet.com
Argyll & Antrim Steam Packet Co.	Campbeltown - Ballycastle	Ferry 165 mins	0870 5523523	www.steam-packet.com

A secondary effect of exporting the Irish pub to all corners of the world, is that the tourists expect to find the same style of pub when they arrive in the country. This has led to many pubs being 'traditionalised' out of all recognition to meet this new trade, and the results are disappointing to say the least. But if you avoid these 'tourist traps' and it's not too difficult, then there's still a lot of 'real Ireland' out there for you to see and explore. In many villages you can still sit down for a pint of Guinness and find yourself in a grocery store, leaning against a cobbler's workbench, or surrounded by bicycle spares.

However, lets assume you can eventually drag yourself away from the bar.

FITZGERALD'S 'IRISH PUB' IN AVOCA

Ireland has some magnificent scenery and there's an almost mystical and timeless quality about the landscapes that unfold around you as you travel around the country. In the north the Giant's Causeway is a 'must see', in fact the whole of the Antrim coastline between Coleraine and Larne is worthwhile exploring, and if you can make it up into the mountains along some of the very dodgy roads in the area, then the views across the Irish Sea to the Scottish coast are magnificent. Heading west and into Eire, the whole of County Donegal is like stepping backwards in time, and there's a scenic experience around almost every bend in the road. To see the wilder parts of the country, then Connemara on the west coast cannot be bettered. Further south, you should take in Dingle, the Ring of Kerry, the Beara Peninsula and Bantry Bay, and if you're not suffering from visual overload after all that then you can take the road through Killarney National Park, but only if you don't mind the crowds. If you must do the 'tourist thing' then there's Blarney Castle and its infamous stone to the northwest of Cork and don't forget the Wicklow mountains south of Dublin and the roads around Loughs Derg, Allen, Erne, Key, Arrow, Corrib and Mask, to name but a few.

You can still park on double yellow lines - sometimes

Accommodation and Information

In the cities and large towns you'll find the usual selection of big hotels, although only a few of the major international chains have managed the trip across the Irish Sea. In the small towns and villages the mainstay of tourist accommodation is the B&B, which is often a private house. Standards range from excellent to the barely acceptable - the same could also be said for some of the landladies - and the price you'll pay is rarely an accurate indicator to the facilities you'll get. But what you do get is contact with the real Ireland and the Irish people, something that you'll never find in a hotel, and a lot of local information that never gets into any of the guide books.

Tourist Board/Information	Website Address
All Ireland Internet Tour Guide	www.allirelandtourism.com
Cavan - the lake county	www.cavantourism.com
Celtic Music & Dance	www.celticcafe.com
County Cork Tourist Guide	www.cork-guide.ie
Hotels in Ireland	www.hotels-europe.com/ireland
Ireland portal site	www.totalireland.com
Ireland's National Tourism Service & portal site for county websites	www.goireland.com
Irish Search - index of all things Irish	www.irishsearch.net
Kerry Tourist Information Centre	www.kerry-insight.com
Northern Ireland Guide	www.guide-to-nireland.com
Northern Ireland Tourist Board	www.discovernorthernireland.com
Proud Irish internet portal site	www.proudirish.com
Softguide Information & Accommodation Booking Service	www.softguides.com/ireland
Tourism Ireland	www.tourismireland.com
Tourism Ireland Travel	www.insight-intermark.com
Tourist Guide Ireland	www.touristguideireland.com
Travel Ireland Accommodation Service	www.travelireland.org

Roads and Routes

Irish roads should be approached with more than a degree of caution! Some would say scepticism would be more appropriate.

They have a reputation for variable surface qualities and just because you're on a good bit don't expect it to last, or even give you any kind of warning when it changes. You could well find a sudden demarcation line between a smooth tarmac road and a potholed farm track just round the apex of that next corner, and if you do, then getting fired four inches out of the seat of your bike at 70 mph is the least of your worries.

However, since 1998 there's been considerable investment in road improvements and resurfacing, so things are getting better - on the main routes at least. Off the beaten track, things are still likely to be just the same. It's worth remembering that in spite of the Irish economic boom that's being driven from the cities and major towns, the rest of the country is still largely agricultural, so keep a good look out for tractors, farm animals and mud and gravel that's run off from the fields. Ireland's also becoming a mecca for backpackers and walkers, so keep an eye open for pedestrians even in the remotest parts of the countryside.

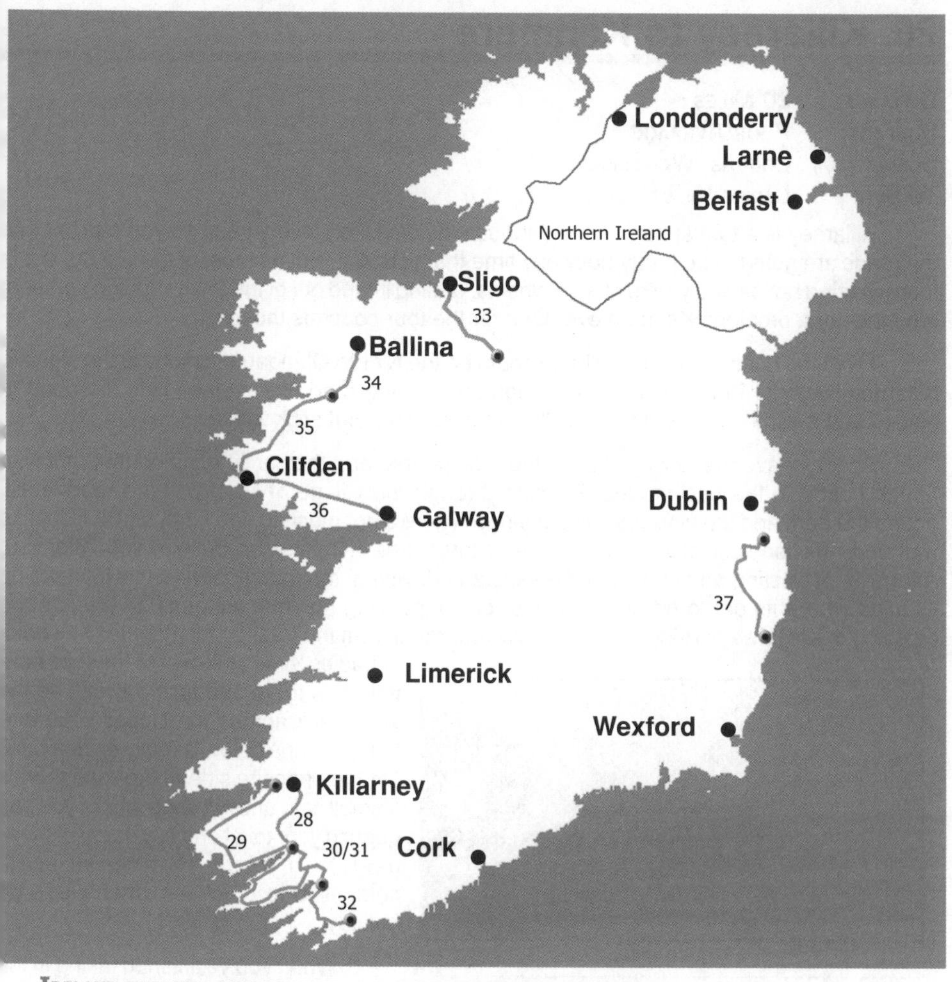

IRELAND SHOWING APPROXIMATE LOCATIONS OF MAJOR TOWNS AND THE ROUTES IN THIS GUIDE

28. Killarney to Kenmare

Distance: 20 Miles
Surface: Poor/Average
Scenery: Loughs, Woodland
To See: Ladies View

Killarney is a tourist trap and has thousands of visitors every year, so you can bet that the roads are going to be pretty busy any time that you visit. But as most of the visitors are in four-wheeled boxes and you're on two-wheels, getting in and out of the town shouldn't present too much of a problem. Keep an eye open for the tour coaches though.

From the centre of Killarney head south on the N71 to Glengarriff, following the signs to Killarney National Park. This is a very narrow, winding road, the surface isn't too good in places and it carries a lot of tourist traffic in the season. But stick with it.

As you leave the town you pass the race course and the castle ruins on the right with Lough Leane in the background. Passing through the village of Muckloss the road finally enters the park and the wooded surroundings. There's not much to see here, which is just as well since the condition of the road and the usual volume of traffic will require all your attention. After a lot of twisting and turning and upping and downing, the road finally seems to make up its mind where its got to go and begins to climb, passing the Torc waterfall on the left and crossing over Galways Bridge before finally emerging from the trees to the popular viewpoint at Ladies View. Pull over to the right here if there's room and take a break as the view back across the Upper Lake and Lough Leane below is really exceptional. On the opposite side of the road there's a small cafe and gift shop where you can quench your thirst and buy some of those useful (?) things that we all seem compelled to purchase when we're on holiday.

Ladies View

When you've finished taking in the sights, it's time to get back in the saddle and continue on the road to Kenmare. After a couple of miles you'll leave the National Park behind, but you're still climbing as the road heads up to the pass at Moll's Gap. From here it's all downhill, and the route descends steadily to the small town of Kenmare, giving excellent views down the river estuary. There's a petrol station and a cafe here, not to mention a wonderful view down the Kenmare Estuary to the sea, that's flanked by the hills of the Beara Peninsular on the left and the mountains of County Kerry on the right.

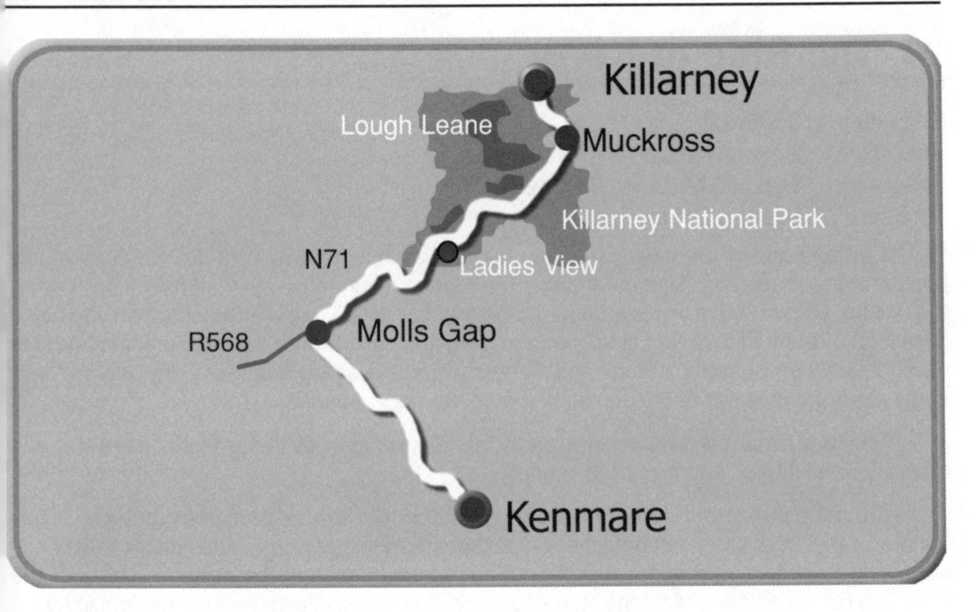

Road	Direction	Comment
N71	Glengarriff Killarney Park	Follow the signs for the Killarney National Park passing the castle with Lough Leane in the background on your right
N71	Glengarriff	Viewpoint at Ladies View is worth a break
N71	Glengarriff Kenmare	Head up to the pass at Moll's Gap and then downhill all the way to Kenmare
		Petrol and refreshments at Kenmare and an outstanding view down the estuary

29. The Ring of Kerry

DISTANCE: **85 MILES**
SURFACE: **POOR/AVERAGE**
SCENERY: **LOUGHS, MOUNTS, COASTLINE**
TO SEE: **SUNSET, STONE FORT**

Perhaps one of the most scenic routes in the whole of Eire, and therefore extremely popular with the tourists. This means that the road is going to be busy at most times during the holiday season, but if you start out early in the day or late in the afternoon then you could miss a lot of the traffic. In fact timing your journey to coincide with catching the last hours of daylight between Sheehan's Point and Cahersiveen on a sunny summer's day can give you some memorable views of the sun setting over the north Atlantic.

The road is narrow, twisting, and pretty bumpy in places, so this is no place to set speed records. Just sit back and enjoy the scenery.

From the centre of Kenmare head north on the N71 towards Killarney, but after a few hundred yards bear sharp left onto the N70 signposted 'Ring of Kerry'. The first six miles or so is nothing to write home about, but then the road starts to hug the northern shore of the Kenmare River estuary and things start improving. At Parknasilla the road turns right to follow a small inlet to Sneem, and then heads up into the mountains for three or four miles before dropping back down towards the coast. At Castlecove there's a narrow turning off to the right that will take you two miles up into the hills to the remains of the Staigue stone fort. From here, there are magnificent views south across the river estuary to the Slieve Miskish mountains.

Continuing on the N70 through Caherdaniel, the road starts to climb up towards Sheehan's Point at the end of the Iveragh peninsular before turning sharp right and crossing the mountain ridge at Coomakesta Pass. There's a small car park and viewpoint here on the left of the road, and it's well worth pausing here as the view is superb. The road now drops down into a coastal valley with views across Ballinskelligs Bay to the island of Great Skellig on the left and Lough Currane on the right. North of Ballybrack the road crosses the outflow of the lough and then starts a gentler climb out of the valley, crossing the northern ridge at Kilpeacan. From here there are good views across to Bray Head and Valentia Island. A little further on the road runs through Cahersiveen, the largest town on the route, so take the opportunity to take a refreshment break or top up with petrol.

We're on the home stretch now, and the road runs along the north side of the peninsular giving spectacular views across Dingle Bay. Follow the N70 all the way now to Killorglin and the end of the 'ring'. The last five miles of the route are a bit un-exciting, so if you've got enough time/petrol there's an interesting diversion around Lough Caragh. About a mile past Caragh Bridge take the turn on the right towards Caragh Lake and then after a couple of hundred yards turn right again towards Shanacashel. Follow the road around the shore of the lough and keep heading towards Shanacashel. Go straight on at the cross roads in the village and then one mile further on turn left at the T-junction. Follow this road all the way to Killorglin and the end of the ring.

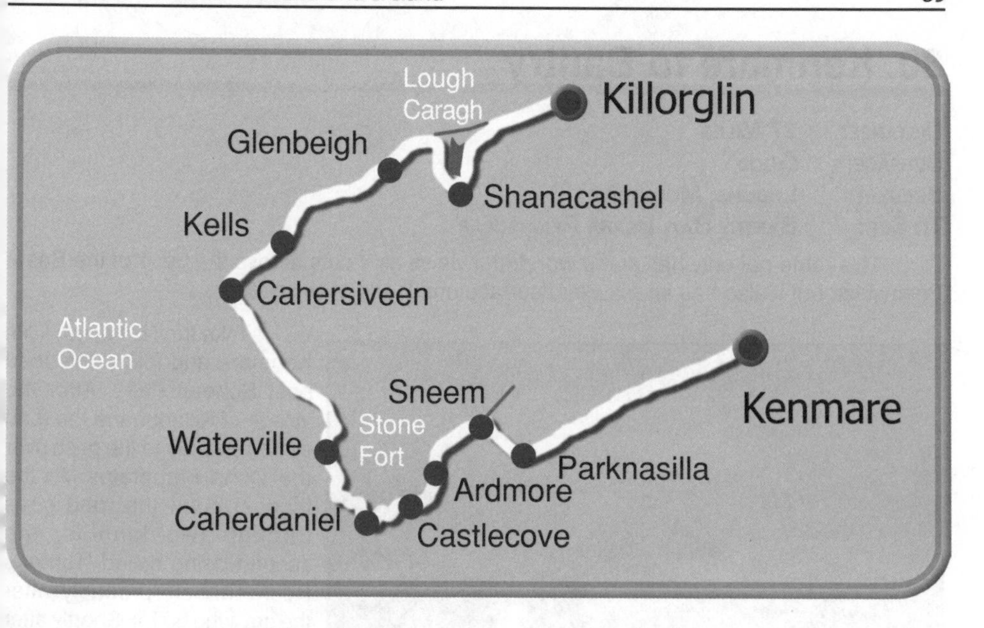

Road	Direction	Comment
N71	Killarney	Head north for a few hundred yards only then bear sharp left
N70	Ring of Kerry	Left onto the N70 along the Kenmare river and follow the Ring of Kerry all the way
N70	Ring of Kerry	Castlecove for views south to Slieve Miskish, great sunsets past Caherdaniel
N70	Ring of Kerry	Cahersiveen for petrol and cafes
Unmarked	Shanacashel	One mile past Caragh Bridge turn right and right again for Caragh Lough.
Unmarked	Killorglin	Straight on at the crossroads in the village and turn left at the T-junction for Killorglin.

30. Kenmare to Bantry

Distance: 27 Miles
Surface: Good
Scenery: Loughs, Mountains
To See: Bantry Bay, Beara Peninsular

This route not only has some wonderful views as it cuts across the base of the Beara Peninsular, but it also has an excellent surface and loads of twisty bits.

By Turner's Rock Tunnel

Take the N71 south from Kenmare and follow this road past Scheen Falls. After the village of Killabunane the road climbs steadily to the pass over the Caha Mountains. At the highest point the road goes through two tunnels, the second being called 'Turner's Rock Tunnel', probably after the guy who built it. Shortly after this the road swings hard round to the left, and there's a viewpoint on the right that gives superb views over Bantry Bay. Follow the twists and turns down into Glengarriff, staying on the N71 and following the signs to Bantry. The road then runs around the base of Bantry Bay, through the village of Ballylickey and on to Bantry. Another good run. In Bantry follow the signs to the seafront. There's plenty of parking around the square by the fountains and the statue of St. Brendan, and the Bantry Bay Hotel is opposite if you need any refreshment.

For the return journey, why not take the coast road around the Beara Peninsular? See Route 31 on the following page.

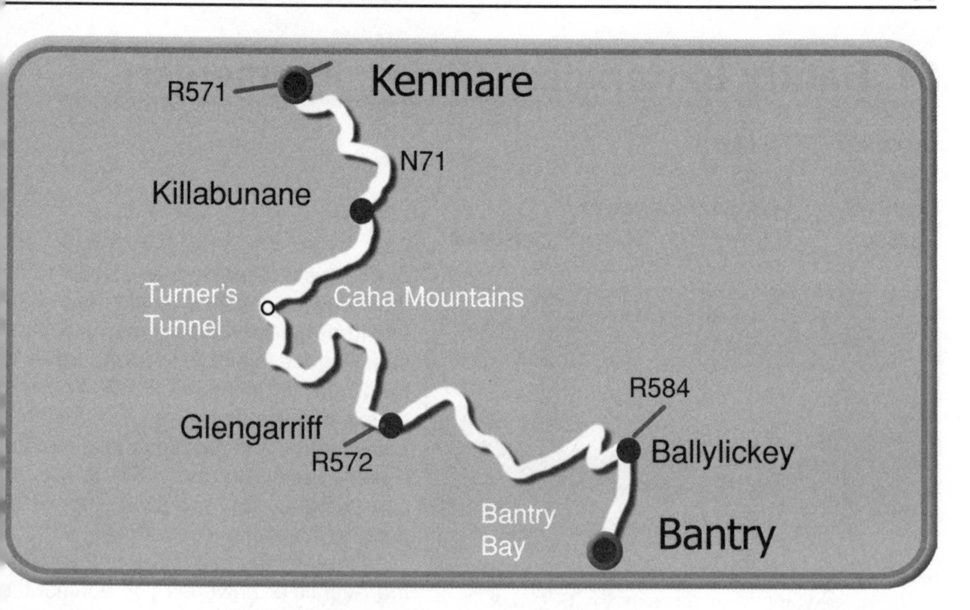

Road	Direction	Comment
N71	Glengarriff	Take the N71 from Kenmare past the Scheen falls and on to Killabunane
N71	Glengarriff	Climb over the Caha mountains and through Turner's Rock Tunnel
N71	Bantry	Follow the road through Glengarriff and Ballylickey to Bantry
		Follow signs to the seafront. Parking in the square by the fountain

31. Bantry to Kenmare (Beara Peninsular)

DISTANCE: **75 MILES**
SURFACE: **GOOD**
SCENERY: **LOUGHS, MOUNTAINS**
TO SEE: **BANTRY BAY, BEARA PENINSULAR**

BANTRY AND THE STATUE OF ST. BRENDAN

This is a spectacular 75 mile route that hugs the coastline as the road twists and turns between the mountains and the sea. Retrace the route to Glengarriff and then bear left onto the R572. Within a couple of miles you're into an altogether more rugged and remote landscape. On a calm sunny day the views to the left across Bantry Bay are awesome; when a storm's brewing it's terrifying, with the wind threatening to either throw you into the Atlantic or pulverise you against the rock faces! The narrow road takes you through the villages of Trafrask, Adrigole and Curryglass to the old working fishing port of Castletownbere, with the mass of Bere Island offering the town some protection from the wild weather that's not uncommon in these parts. Following the R572 takes you through Cahermore and then the road turns north, transforming itself into the R575. There's a turning off to left here that takes you to Dursey Island, but you'll have to leave your bike on the mainland as the only access is by a somewhat rickety cable car.

Staying on the 'main' road you'll pass through Ballydonegan and reach the village of Allilies. This was once a major copper mining centre and over 6000 people lived in the area. Today there are less than 600 and the grey stone towers on the mountainside are all that remain of the mine workings. Running along the edge of Balldonegan Bay, the road turns to the right as it reaches the other side of the peninsular and heads inland towards Kenmare.

Keep on the R575 as it hugs the coastline and then turns inland towards Eyeries, where in true Irish fashion the road transforms itself yet again, this time into the R571. Shortly after leaving Ardgroom you'll pass from Cork back into Kerry, all the while tracking the edge of Kenmare Lough and passing through the villages of Lauragh and Tuosist before rejoining the N71 half-a-mile south of Kenmare.

This is quite a long but worthwhile run, but there are some short cuts shown on the map if you want to return to the bright lights early!

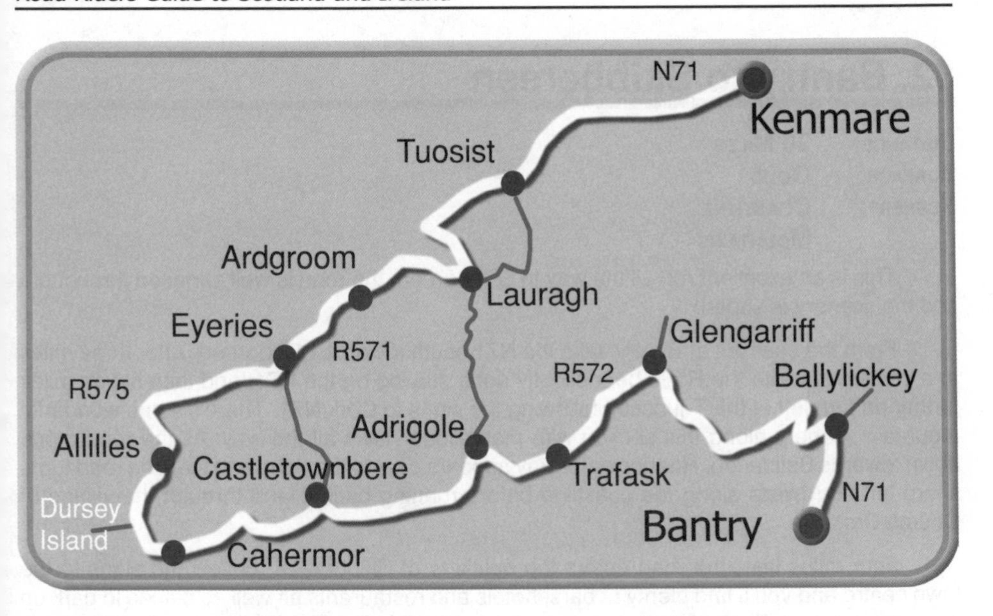

Road	Direction	Comment
N71	Glengarriff	Through Ballylickey and into Glengarriff
R572	Trafask	Turn left onto the R572, follow the road through to Cahermore
R575	Allilies	The R572 becomes the R575. Turn left for Dursey Island if you wish or carry on through Allilies to Eyeries and Ardgroom
R571	Ardgroom	The road becomes the R571 at Eyeries
R571	Kenmare	Through Lauragh and Tuosist to the N71
N71	Kenmare	Follow the N71 into the town

32. Bantry to Skibbereen

Distance: **20 Miles**
Surface: **Good**
Scenery: **Coastline**
Mountains

This is an excellent run all the way to Skibbereen, the road is well surfaced throughout and the scenery is superb.

From the seafront at Bantry, take the N71 south towards Skibbereen. After three miles at a crossroads with the R586 bear slightly right, staying on the N71, and then seven miles further on turn left at the T-junction following the signs to Cork N71. There's some wonderful mountain scenery along this section with marvellous views all the way. As the road drops down towards Balldehob, Roaringwater Bay appears over to the right, and then the road turns sharp left and twists along the coastline before running back inland through the village of Church Cross.

Four miles later the road enters the outskirts of Skibbereen. Follow the signs to the town centre and you'll find plenty of bars, hotels and restaurants as well as places to park up and take a break. The potato famine wreaked a terrible havoc here, and in the fifty years between 1911 and 1961 almost half the population left the area because of failing crops and unemployment. Today the town has a bustling air about it.

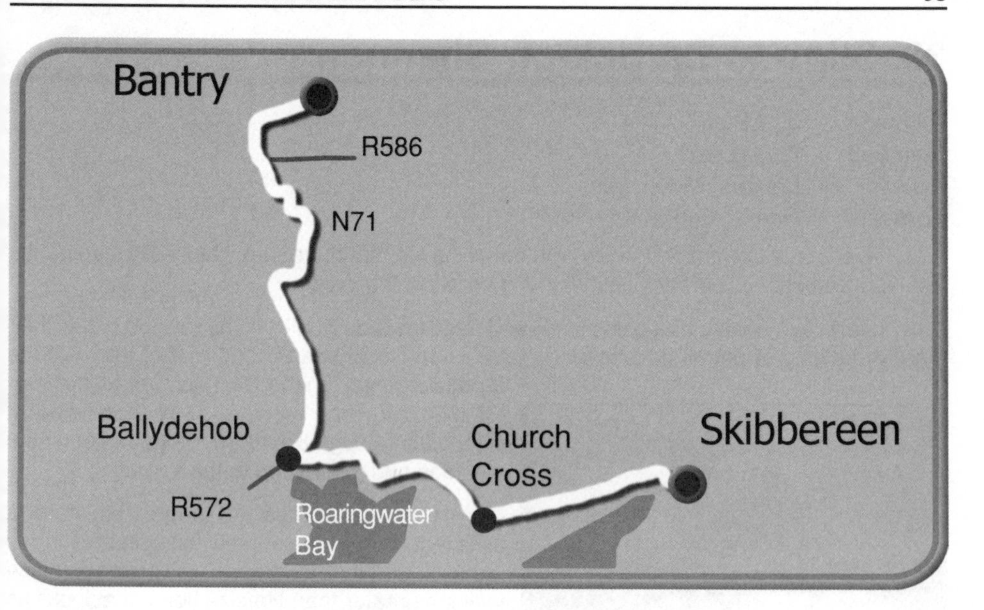

Road	Direction	Comment
N71	Cork	From the seafront at Bantry take the N71 south
N71	Cork	After three miles bear right at the junction with the R586 keeping on the N71
N71	Cork	After a further 7 miles turn right again keeping on the N71
N71	Cork	Through Ballydehob and the views across Roaringwater Bay and on towards Skibbereen
N71	Skibbereen	Follow the signs to the town centre where there are lots of places to take a break

33. Sligo to Carrick-on-Shannon

Distance: 33 Miles
Surface: Excellent
Scenery: Loughs, Mountains
To See: Horse, Lough Key

This is a pretty straightforward run down the N4, but there's an interesting stop on the way and Carrick has a great location on the banks of the river.

Leave the centre of Sligo on the N4 and head towards Dublin. If you're short of fuel then there are plenty of petrol stations along here as the road heads south out of town. At the roundabout stay on the N4, and then at just over 19 miles further on you'll see a viewpoint signposted 'Lough Key View' off to the left. Take this road and follow it up to the carpark.

The Horse

The view across the lough from here is excellent, but perhaps even more interesting is the sculpture in the carpark. It's a strange place to find a greater-than-life-size horse that looks as though it's been put together by a welder working in a scrapyard. It is rather good though.

Head back to the main road and continue on the N4 towards Dublin. This is a major route, busy at times, but wide and well surfaced with good visibility ahead, so it's possible to crack on at a good rate. About ten miles further on, you'll enter Carrick-on-Shannon and as you cross the river bridge, bear round to the right staying on the N4 for Dublin, and there's a useful carpark on the right alongside the river. There's also some even more useful toilets at the far end of the carpark, and a cafe and a few shops a couple of hundred yards away in the town.

Carrick-on-Shannon has all the services that you might require, and if you want to take a break from riding, there's always the possibility of taking a boat out on the river.

Carrick-on-Shannon

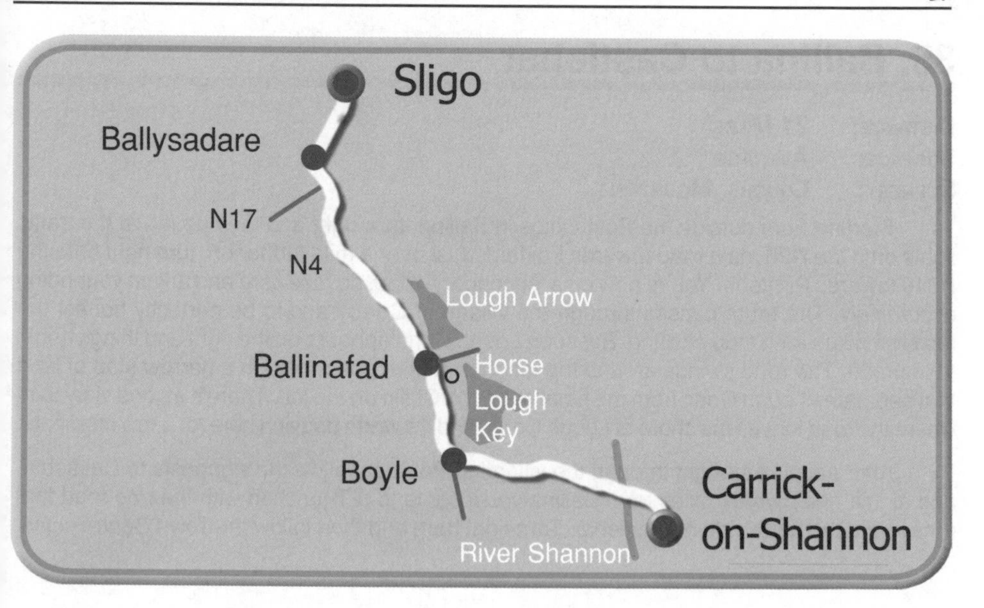

Road	Direction	Comment
N4	Dublin	Leave Sligo on the N4. Stay on the N4 at the roundabout
Unmarked	Lough Key View	Come off the N4 to see the horse and good views of the lough
N4	Carrick	As you enter Carrick-on-Shannon cross the bridge over the Shannon and bear to the right for the car park

35. Ballina to Castlebar

Distance: **21 Miles**
Surface: **Average**
Scenery: **Loughs, Mountains**

Starting from outside the Post Office in Ballina, turn right and then go left at the traffic lights onto the N26 main road towards Foxford. Just over a mile further on, turn right onto the R310 towards Pontoon. You're now on a 'secondary' road, so take care and adjust your riding accordingly. The route passes through the village of Corroy and to be perfectly honest the next few miles aren't too exciting. But soon Lough Conn appears on the right and things begin to improve. The road swings around the lough and then goes through a narrow strip of land that separates Lough Conn from the smaller Lough Cullin on the left. There's a good viewpoint where the road leaves the shore of Lough Conn, and it's worth pausing here for a few moments.

After passing straight through the village of Pontoon follow the signposts to Castlebar, and at just over twenty miles from Ballina you'll come to a T-junction with the ring road that runs round the north side of Castlebar. Turn right here and then follow the Town Centre signs.

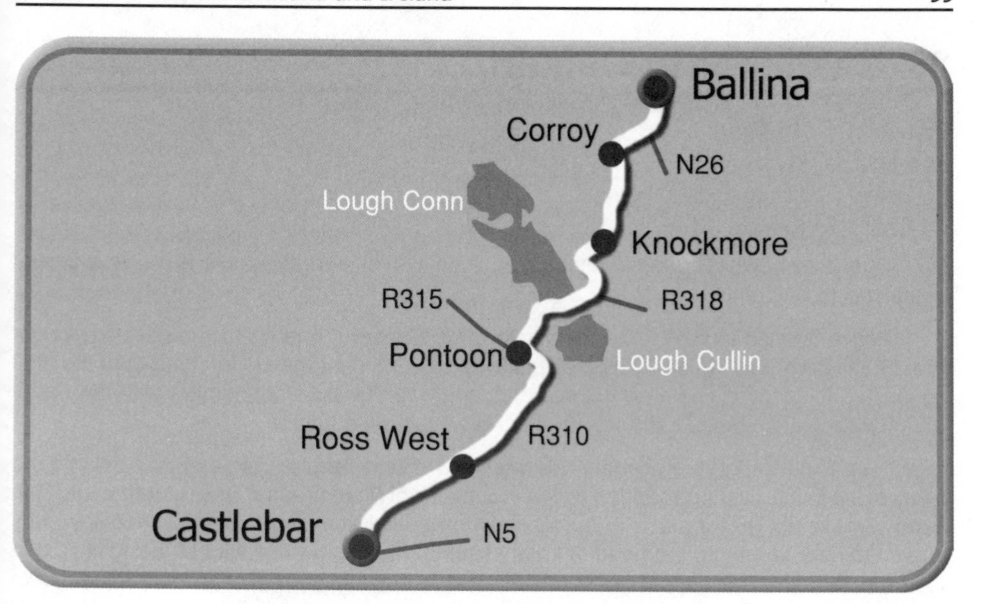

Road	Direction	Comment
N26	Foxford	From the Post Office in Ballina turn right and then left at the lights onto the N26 to Foxford
R310	Pontoon	Turn right onto the A310
R310	Pontoon	Good place to stop between Lough Conn and Lough Cullin
R310	Pontoon Castlebar	Just follow the signs to Castlebar. At the Castlebar ring road turn right and follow the signs for the Town Centre

35. Castlebar to Clifden

DISTANCE: **49 MILES**
SURFACE: **AVERAGE**
SCENERY: **LOUGHS, MOUNTAINS**
TO SEE: **LENANE**

After a somewhat boring first ten miles or so to Westport, this route is a scenic delight all the way to Clifden.

Leave Castlebar on the N5 and head towards Westport, where you should head straight through the centre of the town, over the railway line and past the station, and onto the N59 signposted to Clifden. The road heads south and west towards Connemara with the Partry Mountains away on the left and the Sheffry Hills over to the right.

Past Erriff Bridge the scenery assumes a wild and desolate air, as you pass into the valley of the Erriff River surrounded by the mountains of Maumtrasna, Devils Mother and Ben Gorm. This really isn't a place to break down on a wild and wintry night! The valley ends where the river flows into the head of Killary Harbour, a long narrow inlet of the Atlantic that seems as though it has almost had to force its way in between the hills and looks in danger of being smothered at any moment.

The road follows the water's edge along the south side of the harbour to the small village of Lenane, set at a T-junction and hard up against the Maumturk Mountains in a most amazing setting. There's a pub called the Hamilton Bar, a post office and store, a few houses and a car park. Take a break here and enjoy the solitude of the setting for a moment - if there aren't too many tourists around.

KILLARY HARBOUR AT LENANE

Take the right fork at the T-junction and continue on the N59 along the side of the harbour inlet and around the end of the mountain ridge. The route then heads inland, past a useful petrol station if you're getting a little low, the junction with the R344 and then alongside Kylemore Lough on the left, followed a little further by Kylemore Abbey on the opposite side of the road.

Staying on the N59 will take you alongside Connemara National Park, through Letterfrack, Moyard and Streamstown until you come to a T-junction where you should turn right towards Clifden town centre.

Clifden's a bustling place with plenty of shops, pubs, cafes, restaurants, accommodation and a petrol station, so there'll be no problems in restocking both body and bike.

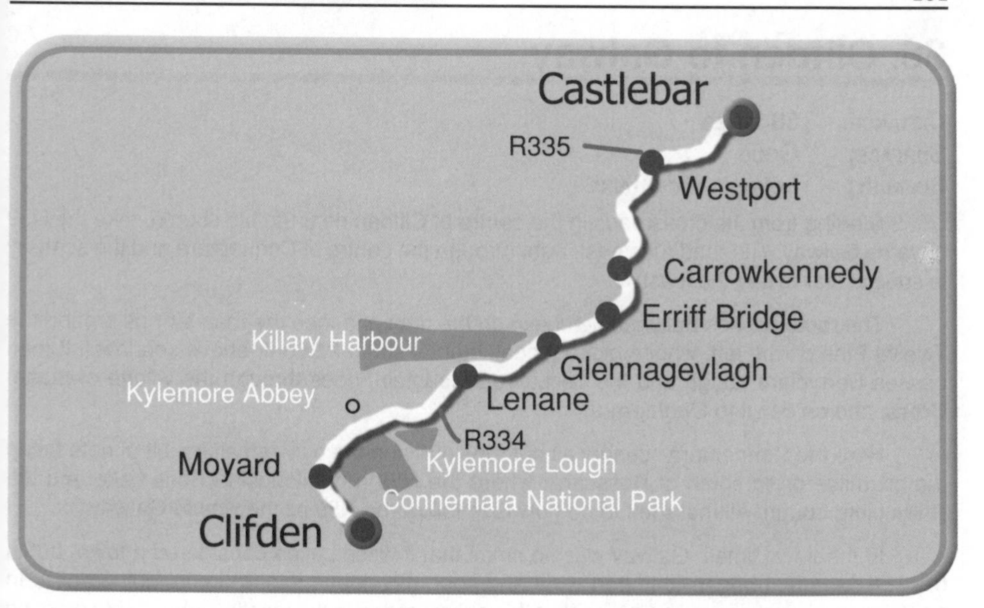

Road	Direction	Comment
N5	Westport	Go straight through Westport and onto the N59
N59	Clifden	Through the Partry and Sheffry mountains
N59	Clifden	Keep on the main road to Lenane
N59	Clifden	Right at the T-junction in Lenane and along the harbour inlet
N59	Clifden	At the T-junction turn right for Clifden town centre where there are sevicves for both rider and bike

36. Clifden to Galway

DISTANCE: 50 MILES
SURFACE: GOOD
SCENERY: LOUGHS, MOUNTAINS

Starting from the crossroads in the centre of Clifden near the big church, take the N59 towards Galway. The road runs east, right through the centre of Connemara and the scenery is spectacular to say the least!

The route passes Ballynahinch Lake on the right and then the road swings around the Twelve Pins on the left, whose highest peak stands some 2,366 ft. above sea level. It then passes Derryclare Lough and the Leckavrea Mountain, goes through the village of Maam Cross, and on down to Oughterard.

Here the Connemara scenery all but runs out, and the only remaining bit of note being the six miles or so south of Rosscahill where the N59 runs alongside Ross Lake and the Ballycuirke Lough. All that's left to do now is to follow the N59 all the way to Galway.

In medieval times, Galway was so small that it wasn't even considered a town, but in the 15th century it began to import wine and soon developed into an important seaport. In 1473 it was almost destroyed by fire, but this only resulted in the wealthy inhabitants erecting lavish properties and the town being rebuilt in a planned manner. Even the introduction of bubonic plague by a Spanish ship in 1649 and the death of over 3,700 of the town's inhabitants couldn't stop the place growing, and nowadays it is one of the fastest growing towns in Europe, fuelled by the technology revolution. However, it has also been described as one of the dreariest towns on the planet. I leave it to you to decide.

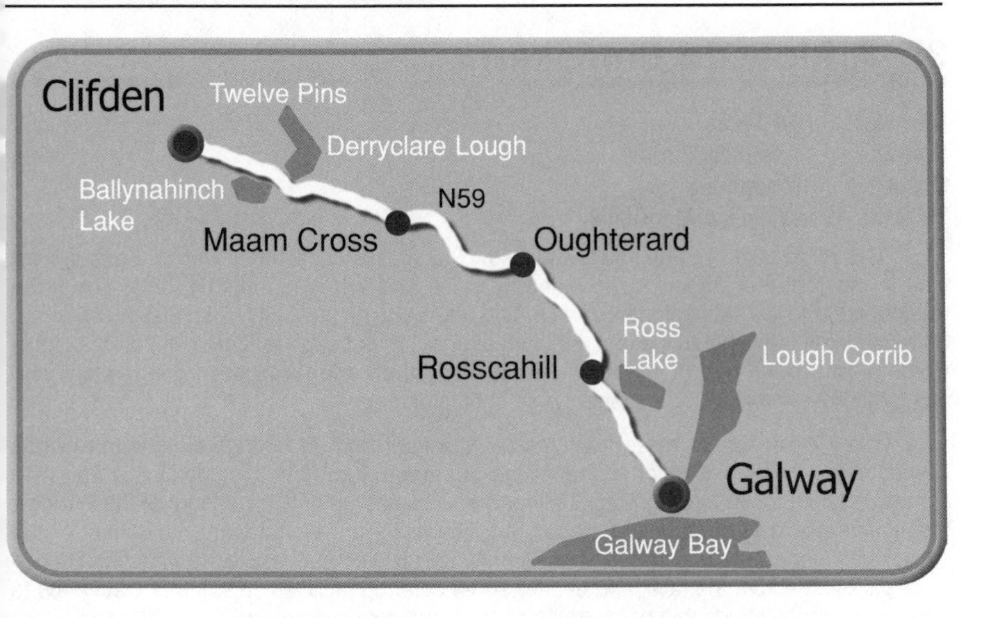

Road	Direction	Comment
N59	Galway	Start from the Crossroads in the centre of Clifden, take the N59 to Galway
N59	Galway	Spectacular scenery all the way to Oughterard
N59	Galway	Just follow the road into Galway

37. Arklow to Enniskerry

Distance: 44 Miles
Surface: Average/Bumpy
Scenery: Mountains
To See: Wicklow Mountains

This route takes you up into the Wicklow Mountains just south of Dublin. From the car park in the centre of Arklow, surrounded by cafes and fast-food emporia, turn right at the roundabout and follow the signs to Avoca. This takes you on the R747. After just over 6 miles, Ballykissangel fans should make a right turn over the river bridge to Avoca and grab a pint in Fitzgeralds, but the rest of you should head straight on and follow the signs to Rathdrum along the Vale of Avoca. The scenery here is outstanding.

At a crossroads 11 miles from Arklow turn right and go through Rathdrum towards Glendalough. At the T-junction in the village of Laragh, turn right towards Dublin and then immediately left towards Sally Gap. The road now climbs up onto the moors of the Wicklow Mountains and is very bumpy in places, but the views are worth every movement of the suspension, especially as you follow the River Avoca up Glenmacnass to the waterfall. There's a car park just above the falls, and usually some catering facilities on summer weekends to refresh the large crowds that come to the area. At the next crossroads up on the moors, turn right towards Dublin and begin the descent down the eastern flank of the mountain. Close to the bottom, turn left towards Enniskerry at the crossroads and follow this road for the next 6 miles. This will bring you to a T-junction where you should turn left towards Enniskerry and Dublin. Keep following the signs to Enniskerry and this will bring you to the centre of the town and it's large central square.

There are plenty of cafes and shops here, as well as a petrol station on the road to Dublin that does first class puncture repairs!

The Waterfall at the Valley of Glenmacnass in the Wicklow Mountains

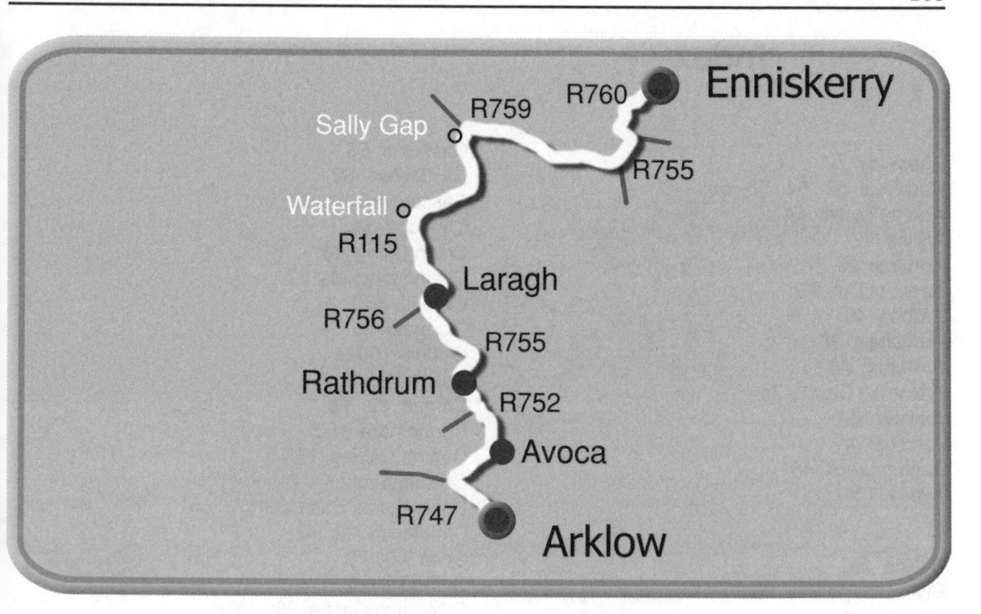

Road	Direction	Comment
R747	Avoca	From the car park in the centre of Arklow take the R747 then the R752
R752	Avoca	Cross the bridge into Avoca and the home of Ballykissangel
R752	Rathdrum	Turn right at the crossroads 11 miles from Arklow onto the R755
R755	Laragh	In Laragh turn right then left towards Sally Gap on the R115. Rest stop at the waterfall
R115	Sally Gap	Turn right at the crossroads on the R759
R759	Dublin	Take the R759 to the crossroads and turn left onto the R755
R755	Dublin	At the crossroads turn left onto the R760 towards Enniskerry
R760	Enniskerry	Follow the road into Ennsikerry

Index